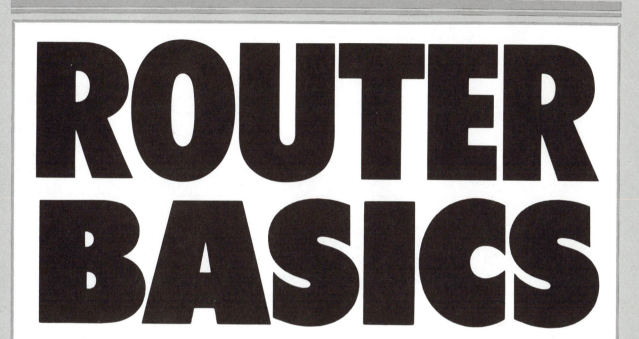

ROUTER BASICS

Patrick Spielman

 Sterling Publishing Co., Inc.   New York

Metric Equivalents

INCHES TO MILLIMETRES AND CENTIMETRES

MM—millimetres   CM—centimetres

Inches	MM	CM	Inches	CM	Inches	CM
⅛	3	0.3	9	22.9	30	76.2
¼	6	0.6	10	25.4	31	78.7
⅜	10	1.0	11	27.9	32	81.3
½	13	1.3	12	30.5	33	83.8
⅝	16	1.6	13	33.0	34	86.4
¾	19	1.9	14	35.6	35	88.9
⅞	22	2.2	15	38.1	36	91.4
1	25	2.5	16	40.6	37	94.0
1¼	32	3.2	17	43.2	38	96.5
1½	38	3.8	18	45.7	39	99.1
1¾	44	4.4	19	48.3	40	101.6
2	51	5.1	20	50.8	41	104.1
2½	64	6.4	21	53.3	42	106.7
2	76	7.6	22	55.9	43	109.2
3½	89	8.9	23	58.4	44	111.8
4	102	10.2	24	61.0	45	114.3
4½	114	11.4	25	63.5	46	116.8
5	127	12.7	26	66.0	47	119.4
6	152	15.2	27	68.6	48	121.9
7	178	17.8	28	71.1	49	124.5
8	203	20.3	29	73.7	50	127.0

Library of Congress Cataloging-in-Publication Data

Spielman, Patrick E.
    Router basics / by Patrick Spielman.
        p.   cm.
    Includes index.
    1. Routers (Tools)   2. Woodwork.   I. Title.
TT186.S667   1990
684′.083—dc20   90-40301
                                       CIP

    7   9   10   8

Sterling ISBN 0-8069-7222-X

Contents

Acknowledgments   4

Introduction   5

1   Exploring the Router   6

2   Bits   23

3   Safety Techniques   35

4   Basic Cutting Guidelines   40

5   Making a Workbench   54

6   Making Straight and Square Cuts   64

7   Making a Bookcase   70

8   Router Tables   78

9   Routing Circles and Arcs   98

10   Basic Template Routing   105

11   Freehand Routing   120

Index   127

ACKNOWLEDGMENTS

A very hearty thank-you is expressed to the following individuals and their companies, who have provided important and expedient assistance to me in a variety of ways: Jim Brewer of Freud U.S.A.; Richard Byrom of Byrom International Corp.; Chris Carlson of Robert Bosch Power Tool Corp.; Nick Cimmarusti of Makita U.S.A., Inc.; Paul Fitzmaurice of Black & Decker; Dennis Huntsman and Kim Thompson Park of Porter-Cable Corp.; Robert Marshall of Jepson Power Tools; Alan Nielson of Ryobi America Corp.; Aki Nozaki of Hitachi Power Tools U.S.A., Ltd.; Steve and Mark O'Brien of Onsrud Cutter, Inc.; Robert Spielman of Spielman Manufacturing; Robert Steck and Charles Van Winkle of Sears, Roebuck and Co.; Dave Tatum of AEG Power Tool Corp.; Jerry Wright of Milwaukee Electric Tool Corp.; and Rick Yorde of Skil Power Tools. I was also totally dependent upon two extremely helpful individuals for their very special talents: Mark Obernberger for superb, quick drawings, and Julie Kiehnau, my editor-typist, who always makes my work look good.

INTRODUCTION

The portable electric router can be an extremely useful workshop aid. But first, the person using the tool has to learn certain basic information. Once he does, his confidence will increase, and he'll soon learn how to master this amazing tool.

Router Basics is written for the amateur woodworker and the first-time router user. It will also prove helpful to those who have occasionally used a router but do not get satisfying results.

One manufacturer estimates that about 60 percent of all routers sold today are used only once, and some not ever at all. If this figure is at all accurate, it is very distressing. It means that some woodworkers have not been able to take full advantage of the tool. If used properly, your

These surface cuts, all from the same board, were made by four different tools. The cuts, from top to bottom, were made by an inexpensive router, a band saw, a table saw, and a handsaw. Note how smooth the router cut is.

router will be the most dependable tool in the workshop.

Router Basics first examines the types of router available, and their features. Advice is given on how to select routers and bits.

Guidelines are given on hand-held routing techniques. Safety is always stressed, so that the novice will know everything about controlling the tool before the bit ever touches the wood.

One of the most effective and entertaining ways to teach technique is through projects. Therefore, I've introduced several interesting projects for beginners. They have easy-to-understand building instructions and step-by-step photos. The skills you can learn on these projects can be applied to many other woodworking projects.

The projects are designed to be made from inexpensive construction-grade lumber you can buy locally. They are very practical, and include a sturdy workbench, an adjustable bookcase, a pegboard, signs, and picture frames.

I also include instructions on how to easily make accessories that will expand the capabilities of your router. This includes two simple squaring jigs. (Jigs are aids that will help you perform a particular technique more easily.) With these jigs you can make perfect square-end trimming cuts, as well as grooves or dadoes that are precisely square to an edge.

One accessory that I'm sure you will find very useful is a router table that can be made very quickly and for just a few dollars. You'll find, as many have, that there are many advantages to using a router table.

This book will guide the beginner through a series of selected procedures that are safe, fun, economical, and inspiring. From this, I am confident that the reader will discover more advanced and expanded uses for woodworking's most popular and practical tool.

Chapter I

EXPLORING THE ROUTER

A router is a portable power tool that has a cutting instrument—called a bit—that cuts the surface or edge of wood. It is perhaps the most versatile woodworking tool because it can make a wide variety of cuts.

There are many different types of router. (See Illus. 1-1.) But don't let this distress you. Once you learn how a router functions, you will be able to pick one that will do what you expect it to do.

In general, routers are described according to either horsepower or the maximum-size opening of their collets, the part which grips the shank (or

Illus. 1-1. *A sampling of the variety of routers available today. Routers range in cost from about $50 to almost $600. Their overall quality, features, and performance capacities also vary greatly. By reading about the different parts of the router and using the buying guidelines included in this chapter, you will be able to buy one that performs well at a price you can afford.*

shaft) of the router bit. (See Illus. 1-2.) Sometimes routers are described by their speed, which is designated by revolutions per minute (RPM). For example, a router may be described as a Sears ¼-inch, 1-horsepower router. "Sears" is the name of the manufacturer. "¼ inch" describes the size of the collet opening.

Types of Router

Routers can be categorized into two distinct groups: *fixed-base* (or standard) routers and *plunge* routers. (See Illus. 1-3 and 1-4.) Fixed-base routers date back to the early 1900s. Plunge routers have been around approximately 30 years.

Fixed-base routers have a motor unit that must be clamped or held vertically within their base before the power is turned on. The essential parts of a typical, inexpensive fixed-base router are shown in Illus. 1-5 and 1-6.

The motor unit on most, but not all, fixed-based routers can be removed from the base. (See Illus. 1-8.) One advantage of having a router with a removable motor unit is that it can be used on commercial (store-bought) or homemade accessories for other routing techniques.

The major disadvantage of a router with a fixed-base design is that the router cannot guide the bit so that it enters into the work surface in a perfectly vertical direction. (See Illus. 1-9.) Fixed-base and plunge routers perform about equally well when it comes to shaping or decorat-

Base   The part of the router that either supports or holds the router's motor unit.

Bit (also called a cutter)   The rotating cutting tool used with a router.

Collet   The part of the router that grips the bit's shank.

Concentric   One or more circles within each other having the same (common) center point.

Depth of Cut   The amount of stock the bit is allowed to cut when either vertically or horizontally controlled with an adjustment or accessory.

Fixed-Base Router   A router that keeps the bit at one fixed vertical position throughout the operation.

Plunge Router   A router which features safe vertical bit movement with the power on. It is essentially employed at the start (entry) and at the completion of the operation.

Router Table   Any routing system in which the router is mounted upside down beneath a flat surface (table) so that the bit protrudes vertically through this surface.

Shank   The rounded shaft of a bit clamped into the router and held by the collet.

Spindle Lock   A device on the router shaft or collet that prevents rotation while installing or changing bits.

Straightedge Guide   An accessory that attaches to the router base. It helps maintain the cutting direction of the router in a continuous straight line.

Sub-Base   A thin piece of smooth plastic attached under the base. It is the surface of the router that rides on the wood workpiece.

Template-Following Guide   A hollow (tubular) accessory attached to the base or sub-base to help control the router while it is being used to duplicate-rout irregular patterns and shapes.

Try Square   A small, non-adjustable tool used to lay out and check 45- and 90-degree corners and angles.

Workpiece   A piece of wood (board) that is either a project component or a suitable piece of scrap used for making a practice cut.

Table 1. *A clarification of terms that are used in this chapter.*

Illus. 1-2. *The parts shown on this fixed-base router are essentially the same parts that can be found on plunge routers.*

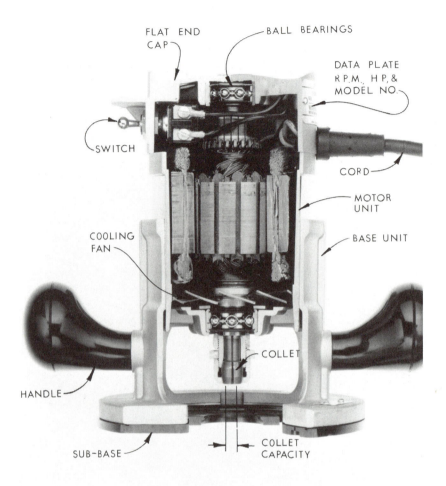

FLAT END CAP

BALL BEARINGS

DATA PLATE R.P.M., H.P., & MODEL NO.

SWITCH

CORD

MOTOR UNIT

BASE UNIT

COOLING FAN

COLLET

HANDLE

SUB-BASE

COLLET CAPACITY

Illus. 1-3. *Two high-quality 1½ horsepower routers with ¼-inch bit shank capacities. At left is a Black & Decker 25,000 r.p.m. fixed-base router. At right is a Hitachi variable-speed plunge router.*

Illus. 1-4. *These two routers differ in many ways. The Sears router on the left, about 1/10 the cost of the Bosch model, is a light-duty model that has a plastic fixed base and 5/8 horsepower, and cuts at a speed of 25,000 r.p.m. (revolutions per minute). The Bosch 3-horsepower model on the right is a heavy-duty plunging router that can cut at different speeds.*

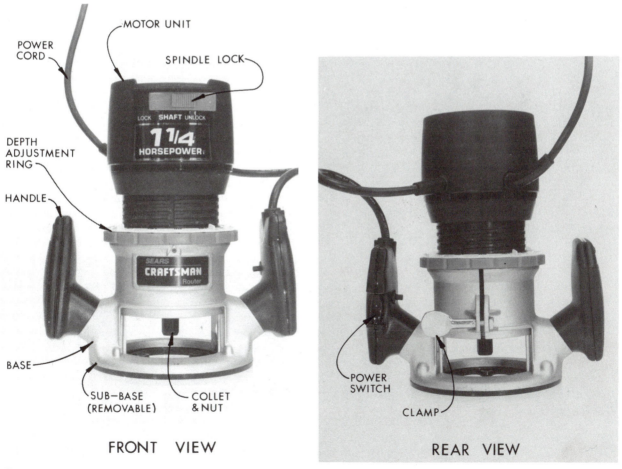

FRONT VIEW

REAR VIEW

Illus. 1-5. *The front view of a typical inexpensive fixed-base router.*

Illus. 1-6. *The rear view of a typical inexpensive fixed-base router.*

Illus. 1-7. *Shown here are the two major parts of a fixed-base router. At left is the motor barrel. At right is a handled holder (base).*

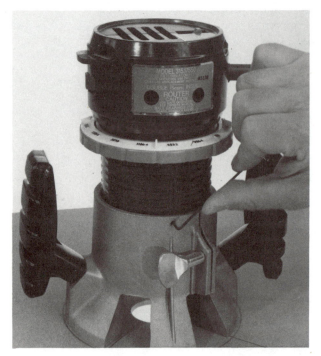

ing the edges of boards (called edge-forming). This is because in edge-forming the rotating bit is brought into contact with the wood from a horizontal feeding direction, rather than vertically, to make the cut. (See Illus. 1-10.) Illus. 1-11–1-14 show the variety of fixed-base routers available today.

Almost all of the routers that have entered the market in the last decade have been plunge routers. Some of these routers are more powerful and have more advanced features. And, even bigger and more advanced plunge routers are expected from router manufacturers.

Illus. 1-8 (left). *To remove the motor unit from the base on some Sears routers, you have to remove a set screw, as shown here. Note: Not all fixed-base routers feature easy removal of their motors.*

Illus. 1-9. *When you are using fixed-base routers, you have to first tilt them on their bases with the power on so that the rotating bit will clear the work surface. Then lower the router to enter the bit into the work surface. It is obvious that for this class of work, fixed-base routers are more awkward and hazardous and less accurate than plunge routers.*

Illus. 1-10. *Fixed base routers (shown here) and plunging routers perform about equally well when forming or shaping the edges of boards. In this kind of work, the router brings the rotating bit into the work from a horizontal direction, rather than from a vertical direction.*

Illus. 1-11. *A look at some routers that are relatively inexpensive. The two on the left in the front row are made entirely of plastic.*

Illus. 1-12. *These fixed-base routers have different construction features. For example, the openings in their bases are of different sizes.*

Illus. 1-13. *These high-quality fixed-base routers are much sturdier than those shown in Illus. 1-11, and have motors with greater horsepower.*

Illus. 1-14. *These fixed-base routers are called laminate trimmers. They are generally used to trim the plastic material used on cabinet counter tops. However, because they are small and portable, they are useful for many light-duty routing jobs, such as model work and shallow sign or engraving work. The router on the left is manufactured by Ryobi, and the two on the right by Porter-Cable.*

Plunge routers have their motor units vertically adjustable on two spring-loaded posts attached to a base. (See Illus. 1-15 and 1-16.) This means operating motor units can be moved safely up and down on the posts. The operator can lower the rotating bit vertically into the workpiece squarely, at exactly 90 degrees to the surface. Once the pre-set depth of the cut is reached, the motor and bit are locked at that height. After the cut is completed, the spring-loaded motor unit is released. It rises, automatically retracting the bit safely back above the base and out of the work. (See Illus. 1-17.)

FRONT VIEW

Illus. 1-15. *The front view of a typical plunge router, showing its essential parts.*

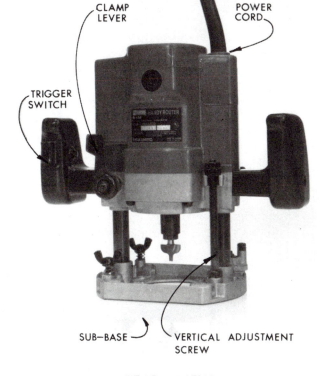

REAR VIEW

Illus. 1-16. *The rear view of a typical plunge router, showing its essential parts.*

Illus. 1-17. *A plunge router can bring the bit directly into and out of the work in a perfectly vertical direction.*

Currently, there are not many plunge routers available that are inexpensive. Illus. 1-18 shows a variety of ¼-inch plunge routers. The description "¼ inch," as mentioned earlier, refers to the diameter of the collet opening.

Many manufacturers sell both fixed-based routers and plunge routers. Ryobi and Porter-Cable are two manufacturers who have basically combined the design features of the fixed-base and the plunge routers. Both sell one version of a plunge router that has a removable motor unit.

Important Parts and Features

Collet

As mentioned, the *collet* is the clamping system on the end of the motor shaft that grips the bit.

(See Illus. 1-19–1-21.) It is a very important part of the router, and your router must have a good one.

Generally, the longer the collet, the better the bit is supported. This makes the bit rigid, which reduces vibration and chatter in the cut. And, of course, the collet should be made from sufficiently hard or treated steel so that it doesn't wear out.

Some of the collets on lower priced routers have to be replaced after moderate usage. They wear out quickly. Some even develop oval-shaped openings rather than maintaining perfectly round inside openings.

Clamping and Locking Mechanisms

Clamping and locking mechanisms are those devices on a router that lock the motor in a vertical position, and which place a bit at a certain depth

Illus. 1-18. *A selection of ¼-inch plunge routers made by different manufacturers. Note the variety of handle styles, the different types of switch, and the different base designs.*

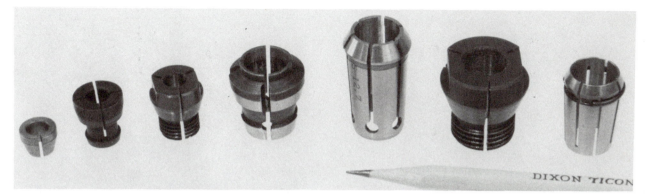

Illus. 1-19. Collets are the clamping system on the end of the motor shaft that grips the bit. They vary in size and design from manufacturer to manufacturer. Short collets, like the three shown on the far left, are usually found on light-duty routers. They do not keep the bit as rigid or as true while it is ro- tating; thus, there is more vibration and the cuts are rougher. Longer collets are better. Some collets are designed to spring open when loosened. This helps prevent the bits from sticking inside collets, and leads to quick bit changes.

Illus. 1-20. The collets on Sears routers are bored into the end of the slotted and threaded motor shaft.

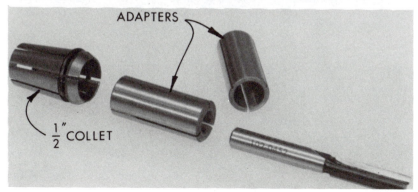

Illus. 1-21. Bigger routers with collets that have a ½-inch diameter can be fitted with steel or fibre adapters so that smaller-diameter bit shanks (⅜ and ¼ inch) can be used.

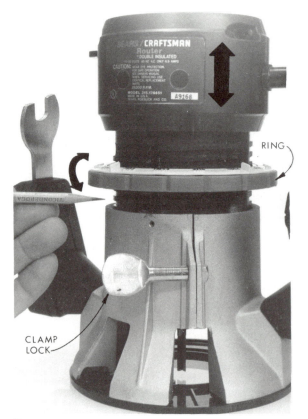

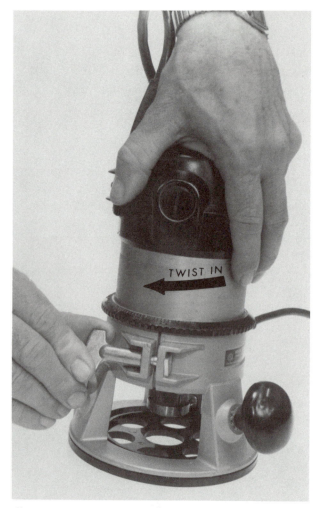

Illus. 1-22. *The motor in the adjustment ring system cannot be changed as quickly when there is a major change in the depth of the cut. To use this system, rotate the threaded ring on the motor to raise or lower the bit. Normally, the ring rests on the upper edge of the motor base. For quick, non-precise adjustments, raise the ring sufficiently clear of the base, as shown.*

Illus. 1-23. *Twist or screw-in motor systems, such as on this Porter-Cable fixed-base router, work well to make fine vertical adjustments.*

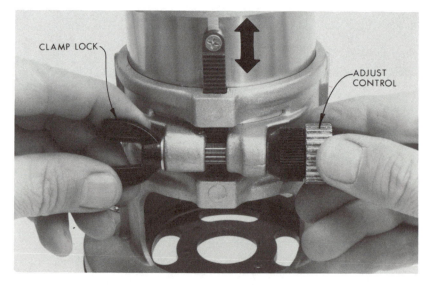

Illus. 1-24. *A rack-and-pinion mechanism makes accurate microadjustments (to the hundredth of an inch) on this Black & Decker fixed-base router quick and easy.*

of cut in the workpiece. They are another very important design element of the router.

The last thing a person using a router wants to worry about is that a clamp or lock is going to come loose. Therefore, locks should have sizable threaded bolts and thumbscrews or levers that are long enough so that the operator can easily lock the motor.

Fixed-based routers have three different ways in which motors are adjustable in the bases. They are: the adjustable ring system (Illus. 1-22), the screw-in (spiral) arrangement (Illus. 1-23), and the rack-and-pinon system (Illus. 1-24). The most important consideration when trying to determine which one to choose is whether it can make fine adjustments (adjustments to a hundredth of an inch) more quickly and easily than the others. Another thing to consider is whether you can make fine adjustments easily when the router is upside down, hanging under a router table.

Plunge routers have different ways of locking the motor. Some have levers intended for left-hand operation. Others have levers intended for right-hand operation. Three different systems are shown and described in Illus. 1-25–1-27. Whichever system you select, it should be able

Illus. 1-26. *This plunge router features a twist-knob plunge lock. Simply rotating the right-hand knob clamps the motor in place. This type of lock takes a while to get used to. You might find yourself inadvertently loosening the clamp when lifting the router or using it.*

Illus. 1-25. *The plunge lock levers on many routers like the one shown here are small and not long enough for easy leverage. Press the lever downwards to lock the motor in position.*

Illus. 1-27. *Some plunge-locking devices are intended for left- rather than right-hand operation, which is a plus for natural left-handers. This Porter-Cable plunger router features a spring-loaded, self-locking clamp lever which automatically locks the motor in place when it is released.*

to clamp the motor unit firmly. However, it should not clamp the unit so firmly that it needs a person with an unusual amount of strength to unclamp it.

Switches and Handles

Routers have a great variety of types of switch. Some are not very effective, and others are not located in an easy-to-reach position. The switch must always be dependable and easy to use.

The router with the best type of switch is one which you can operate while always maintaining a firm, comfortable grip on the handles with both hands. This means that when you start or stop the power, you do not have to reach or search for the switch. Illus. 1-29–1-33 show the different switches and handles available. If you feel at all uncomfortable with your switch, buy an auxiliary foot switch as shown on page 39.

The handles on routers come in many different styles and sizes. I prefer easy-to-grip handles located low, close to the workpiece surface, because such a router is easier to control and feels

Illus. 1-29. *This router has a D-handle, trigger switch, and second safety switch on the motor unit. This is an ideal arrangement for a fixed-based router. With the D-handle, you are certain of a firm grip. To use the trigger switch, simply press the trigger located on the handle.*

Illus. 1-28. *The fine-height adjustment shown here gives precise depth-of-cut control on this router.*

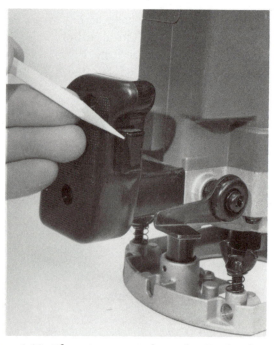

Illus. 1-30. *The trigger switch on this Ryobi plunge router works with a safety lock-off button (not visible). The lock-off button is depressed by the operator's thumb on the inside of the handle before the power trigger switch, indicated by the pencil, will engage. This is another excellent safety feature. Note the plunge lock lever located close to the handle.*

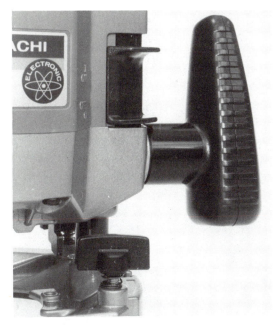

Illus. 1-31. *The switch on this Hitachi router is located near the handle, and slides up and down. The handle can also be tilted, so you can choose the handle position you are more comfortable with.*

Illus. 1-32. *Note the handle and the sliding switch on this plunge router.*

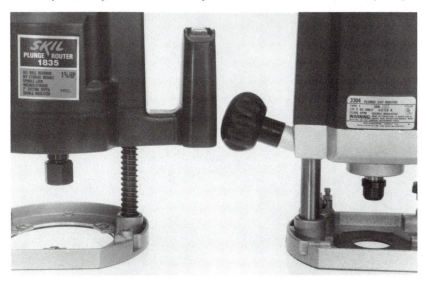

Illus. 1-33. *Compare the different handles, base openings and columns on these two routers. Exposed coil springs, as shown on the router at the left, make posts more difficult to clean and lubricate. The switch on the router at the left is located on the top of the handle.*

better balanced. High handles on some plunge routers give the sensation that the router is tipping.

Bases and Sub-bases

Bases and *sub-bases* are very important parts of the router. Here, again, there are many different types. Some are entirely round, some are square, and some are round with one or two flat edges.

I do not have a preference as to the specific shape of the base or sub-base. However, it should be noted that to make a router truly versatile, you often have to replace the sub-base that comes with it with one of many possible self-made sub-bases that are better suited for the particular job. These sub-bases might be better because they are wider, longer, thicker, more transparent, with bigger or smaller holes, or for other reasons. Sadly, some manufacturers make no provision at all for removing or exchanging sub-bases.

As you progress beyond simple router tasks, you will eventually want to hang your router upside down to make a router table. To do this, you need at least three, preferably four, large threaded sockets in the base housing. Screw-hole sockets for mounting bases or tables are often sub-standard. Most manufacturers do provide some sort of system for attaching special straight-edge guides and template-following guides to router bases. (A straightedge guide is a device that helps you to cut straight. A template-following guide is a device that allows you to cut along a template, which is a full-sized pattern cut from stiff material.)

Illus. 1-34–1-39 compare different types of bases and show their advantages and disadvantages.

Illus. 1-34. *Some routers have bases with big openings. Others have bases with small openings. Small openings give better router base support when you are working on small or narrow pieces and when you are working on the edges of boards at the corners. Large holes give you better visibility when you are following layouts freehand, as in sign work. Also, bits with larger cutting diameters can be used.*

Illus. 1-35. *Most router bases have provision for installing template guides regardless of the size or configuration of the base opening (hole), or whether the sub-base is of the screw-on or non-removable type.*

Illus. 1-36. *Good bases and sub-bases are essential for full router versatility. Several good-sized threaded sockets in the base are needed for do-it-yourself router table setups as well as for attaching various guides and other special bases to the bottom of routers.*

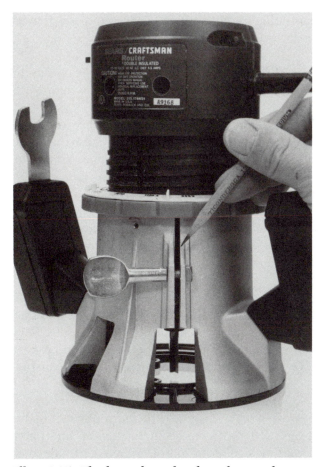

Illus. 1-37. *The base clamp has been loosened to permit vertical adjustment of the motor unit. Note the gap of at least ⅛ inch at the split of the cast-aluminum base. This is indicated by the pencil.*

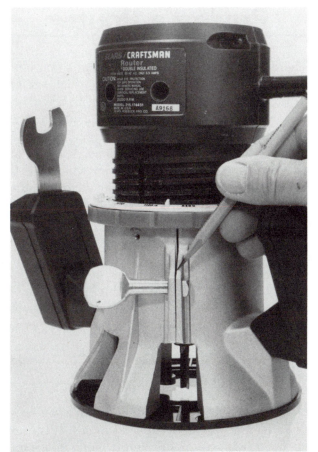

Illus. 1-38. *The base clamp has been tightened. There is now very little gap. This exerts pressure on the thin plastic sub-base, which causes it to buckle slightly. It also makes the outer edges of the sub-base non-concentric to the bit.*

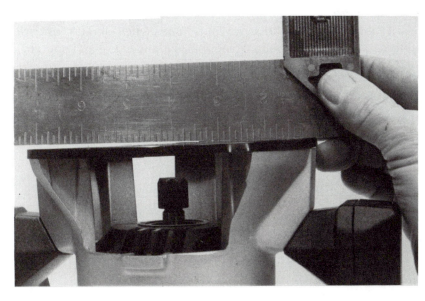

Illus. 1-39. *This try square is being used to check the flatness of the sub-base. As shown, the sub-base has buckled slightly, due to the forces placed upon it when the base clamp was tightened to secure the motor. See Illus. 1-37 and 1-38.*

Buying a Router

There are many things you will have to consider when you are trying to determine which router to buy. Before buying any router, first hold it, test the working parts, and pay close attention to all its features and those previously discussed.

Following are a list of additional features or characteristics you should consider when selecting a router. It will be very difficult to find the ideal router: one that has all the features at a price you can afford, and one which has a very good repair service that guarantees its work. You may decide to buy a less expensive router that has some design deficiencies or not all the features you want. Remember this general rule: The lower the price of the router, the more quickly parts such as bearings and collets wear out.

Following is a list of factors that you should consider before buying a router:

1. *Horsepower*. The horsepower of a router is more important than its speed (r.p.m.). It is usually worthwhile to spend slightly more money for a router that has ¼ or ½ more horsepower.

2. *The noise level of the router*. Though the noise level of a router doesn't affect the way it cuts, it can affect your hearing. Cheaper routers and older models *seem* to run louder. And there is a definite difference in the noise levels of some of the newer routers. (Even if you buy a router that is fairly quiet, it is essential that you wear ear protection. This is discussed in Chapter 3.)

3. *The cord*. A cord can turn out to be a nuisance. Make sure that the router you buy has a cord that is not stiff or undersized, or that is awkward around the router.

4. *Bit changing*. Make sure that it is easy to change bits on the router you are buying.

5. *Collet wrenches*. These are the wrenches used to tighten the collet. Make sure that they are well made and comfortable. The wrench or wrenches that come with some routers can be stored on the router itself.

6. *Spindle lock*. Some routers have a spindle (or shaft) locking mechanism which requires only one wrench for changing bits.

7. *Vibration*. Make sure that the router does not jerk excessively when you turn it on, and that vibration can't be felt through the handles. The router should operate smoothly without excessive slop or play in its adjustment mechanisms.

8. *Accessories*. Make sure that the proper accessories or bits come with the router. Also, be aware that replacement bolts, screws, and parts sometimes come in metric dimensions, and that some may not be obtained locally.

9. *Service*. Make sure that there is a locally available repair service with an inventory of parts.

10. *Instructions*. The seller should provide personal instructions on how to use and operate a router, and provide an owner's manual.

11. *Hands-on testing*. Make sure that you are able to hold, manipulate, and test the working functions of the router before buying it.

Chapter 2

BITS

Even the best-made router will not produce consistently good cuts unless bits of reasonably good quality are used. Bits, after all, are the parts of the router that are actually doing the cutting.

A well-made bit is made of high-quality steel or carbides. It should be machined to precise cutting angles and clearances and have smooth, heat-expelling flutes (flutes remove the chips). Each bit must be perfectly balanced. (See Illus. 2-1).

These important qualities are almost impossible to detect with the naked eye by the first-time bit buyer or even the professional. Thus, be very careful when buying bits or you may end up disappointed.

Router bits are essentially made from one of two materials, or combinations of the two materials. Bits consist of either (1) high-speed steel (sometimes abbreviated as HSS) or (2) high-speed steel with the bit's cutting edges tipped with carbide (ct) or all solid carbide. Carbides stay sharp, about 20 times longer than steel bits, but they are more expensive. Use them for very tough materials like plywood, which would dull high-speed steel quickly.

Overall, high-speed-steel bits have the sharpest edges and cut hardwoods more smoothly, but they do not keep their initial sharpness as long as carbide bits.

The best way to buy bits is either to ask the advice of an experienced woodworker or buy one or two of the long-established brand-name bits and test them yourself. Don't select a bit just because it's inexpensive.

If you are using a router that has less than 1½ horsepower, I suggest starting with high-speed steel, ¼-inch shank bits unless you're cutting some very tough material (like plywood) that will dull the bit.

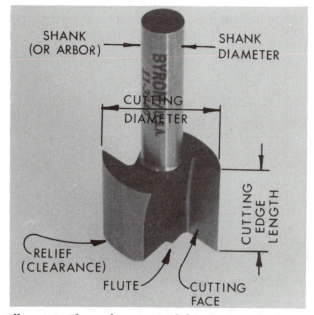

Illus. 2-1. *Shown here is a solid (one-piece) high-speed-steel bit. The size of the bit is determined by the diameter of the shank, cutting edge length, cutting diameter and, frequently, overall length.*

Types of Bit

Bits come in many different sizes and shapes. However, they can be broken down into three general groups according to the type of cut they make. These three general groups are discussed below.

Surface-cutting Bits

Surface-cutting bits, which cut the surface of the wood, can be used to do such jobs as make various-shaped grooves and square dadoes. (See Illus. 2-1–2-3.)

Most surface-cutting bits can enter the wood from a vertical starting direction and proceed

Bead   A small rounded (convex) surface such as can be found on a piece of moulding.

Bevel   An angular-cut surface or edge.

Brazing   A form of welding that secures a carbide cutting edge to a steel router bit.

Carbide   A very hard, long-lasting, but somewhat brittle metal used to make entire router bits, or used just on the cutting edges (tips) of other bits.

Chamfer   The surface resulting from cutting away the angle at the intersection of two faces of a piece of wood.

Core Box Bit   A nonpiloted surface-cutting bit that forms a groove with a rounded concave bottom.

Cutting Diameter   The resulting maximum width of the path made by any router bit at one pass.

Cutting Edge Length   Maximum measurement of the full vertical-cutting capacity of a router bit.

Dado   Square or rectangular recessed channels cut into a wood surface against the grain of the wood.

Feed rate   The speed at which the router is advanced.

Flute   A straight or spiral groove behind the cutting edge of a router bit that permits the chips to be expelled from the cut.

Grooves   Rectangular or square recessed channels cut into a wood surface along the grain direction of the wood.

Hardwoods   Woods with average-to-high impact resistance.

High-Speed Steel   Hardened and treated metal used to make router bits with maximum sharpness.

Keyhole Bit   A router cutter that produces a special slotted groove on the backs of picture frames, etc., to permit objects to be wall-hung.

Laminate Trim Bit   A router cutter with a piloted guide that makes flush cuts to pare down overhanging plastic and wood components.

Mortises   Rectangular holes or slots cut into wood that will receive another member (called a tenon) to make a right-angle joint.

Pitch   A thick, sticky, resinous substance or residue often found in softwoods.

Plywood   A sheet material made by gluing thin layers of wood together with the grain direction of each layer running at right angles to the next one.

Rabbet Bit   One of many kinds of edge-forming bit with a piloted end that makes an L-shaped cut along an edge or end of a board.

Resin   A natural or artificial substance that is not soluble in water.

Roundover Bit   One of the many kinds of edge-forming bit with a piloted end that converts square edges, ends, and corners of a board to a convex radius.

Self-Guiding Bit   A bit that has a noncutting protrusion called a pilot that bears against the edge of a workpiece or pattern to limit its horizontal depth of cut.

Slots   General reference to variously shaped channels such as mortises, dadoes, and grooves that are cut into wood.

Softwood   A term used to describe the physical hardness of various woods with low-to-medium impact resistance.

Spiral Bits   A special type of router cutter with helical or coil-like cutting edges and grooves (flutes) that lift the chips out of the cut.

Tongue-and-Groove Joint   A special type of wood-mating system widely used for wood flooring and wall panelling with male- and female-formed interlocking edges.

Table 2. *A clarification of terms that are used in this chapter.*

horizontally to make the bottom and sides of the cut smoothly and accurately. However, you will need an aid to mechanically guide the router so that the cuts are as accurate as possible. When you have gained some experience, you will be able to do freehand work, work for which you do not need something to guide the router. (Refer to Chapter 11.)

Edge-forming Bits

Edge-forming bits are used to make decorative or functional joint-fitting cuts along the edges of boards. (See Illus. 2-4–2-6).

Edge-forming bits are self-controlling horizontally. They have a piece that extends out of the lower end, called a "pilot." It follows along the edge of the workpiece, either in a straight line or along irregular curves. The pilot controls the amount of material that can be cut away horizontally.

Solid bits with small integral pilots, as shown in Illus. 2-5–2-7, tend to burnish the uncut area of the wood travelled by the pilot. The pilot rotates at the same high speed of the router and bit rotation, causing heat and friction. Bits with ball-bearing pilots (Illus. 2-6) are very popular among craftsmen. This is because ball-bearing pilots do not generate heat caused by friction, as do integral pilots.

Edge-forming bits cannot be used to make

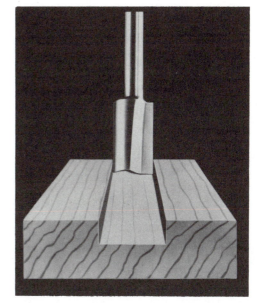

Illus. 2-2. *A typical straight-cutting high-speed-steel bit. Bits of this type are not self-guiding, so you must control the router itself with the aid of some type of accessory. Bits that have ¼-inch shanks range from ⅛ to ¾ inch in cutting diameters.*

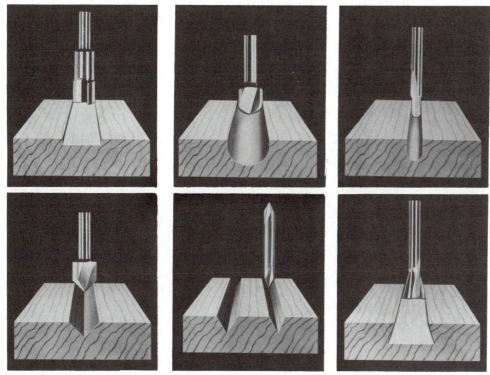

Illus. 2-3. *Some surface- and joint-cutting bits. At top left is a hinge-mortising bit. It is used to cut the mortise (recess) in the door into which the hinge will go. At top center is a core-box bit. The bit on the top right is a veining bit. At the bottom left is a V-groove bit. It makes a groove in the shape of a V. The bit in the middle is a double-end V-groove bit. The one at the far right is a dovetail bit.*

Illus. 2-4. *This edge-forming "rabbeting bit" has a pilot that rides against the edge of the workpiece and controls the horizontal depth of cut. The desired vertical depth of cut is determined and adjusted by the operator. This bit cuts a ⅜-inch-wide rabbet along straight or irregular edges of the workpiece. (A rabbet cut is made along the edge of the board. It forms an L shape.) Rabbet bits are used more for joinery cuts than for decorative cuts.*

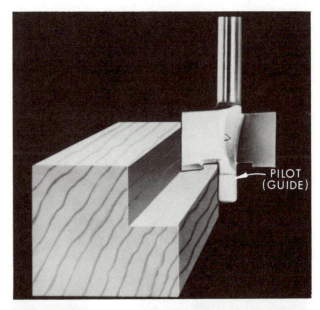

Illus. 2-5 (below). *On the top row are popular edge-forming bits. From left to right, they are a round-over bit, a cove-cutting bit, and a roman ogee bit. On the bottom row, from left to right, are a beading bit, a chamfer bit, and a flush-laminate trimming bit.*

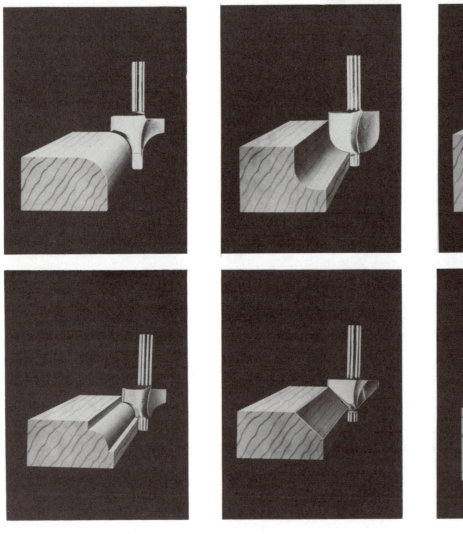

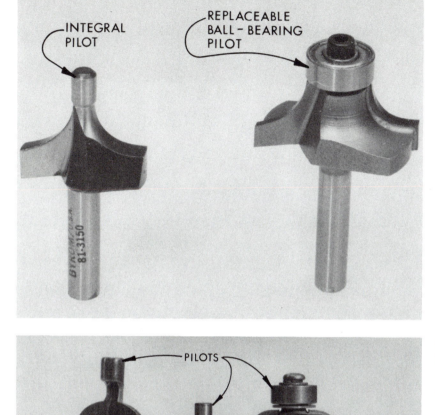

Illus. 2-6. *The round-over bit on the left is made of high-speed steel. It has an integral pilot, which means the pilot is part of the bit. The round-over bit on the right is carbide-tipped. It has a ball-bearing pilot that can be removed.*

Illus. 2-7. *The inexpensive bit at left is made of stamped sheet steel. It can be used only for shallow (⅛-inch) cuts in hard wood. The high-speed-steel bit in the middle will give the sharpest edge, but dulls quickly when used on tough material like plywood. The carbide-tipped bit on the right is more expensive. It is the most durable. It stays sharp 20 times longer than steel. It cuts all materials well. The pilot on the carbide-tipped bit is a replaceable ball bearing.*

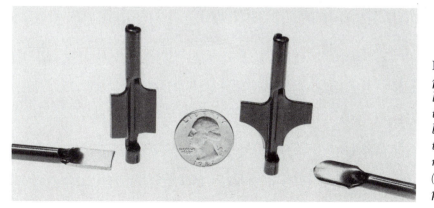

Illus. 2-8. *A look at several inexpensive stamped-steel bits. These bits come in many different cutting shapes. However, they have limited use on woods that are tough to cut. To use these bits, make successive shallow cuts (⅛ inch deep) until the desired profile or depth is reached.*

Illus. 2-9. *Here is a good set of bits for the beginner to use. All are one-piece, high-speed-steel bits. They all have ¼-inch-diameter shanks. From left to right, they are: ¼-inch straight bit, ½-inch-cutting-diameter core box, ¼-inch-radius cove bit, ⅜-inch-radius round-over bit, and ⅜-inch rabbet.*

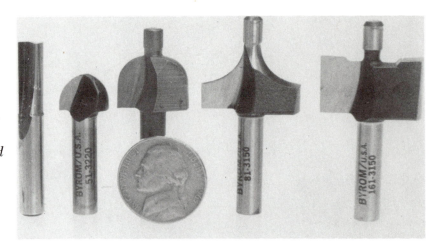

cuts on the surface of the wood. Sometimes, however, surface-cutting bits can be guided along the edge of a board. For example, you can use a straight-cutting bit to make a rabbet cut if you use a guide-fence accessory to guide the cut.

Illus. 2-9 shows high-speed-steel bits that would make a good set for the beginner. Illus. 2-11–2-13 show bit sets you may want to consider buying once you have gotten some experience. Included in these sets are some straight-cutting bits of various diameters. Remember, it is possible to make wide cuts with bits that have smaller diameters if you make two or more passes at different settings. However, it is impossible to cut a ¼-inch-wide groove if all you have is a ⅜-inch-wide bit.

Always use the biggest bit possible. It will cut smoother and have less vibration or "chatter" than bits with smaller cutting diameters.

Illus. 2-14–2-16 show and describe what a beginner should look for when he is buying his first carbide-tipped bits. One very useful carbide-tipped bit is a straight-cutting bit that has a ball-bearing guide (Illus. 2-17). Another is a ¼-inch solid carbide spiral bit. Solid carbide bits are made entirely of carbide. They were very expen-

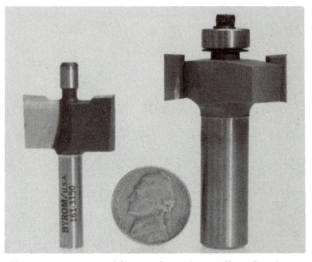

Illus. 2-10. *Two rabbeting bits that will make the same-size cuts. The one on the left is a high-speed-steel bit with a ¼-inch shank. The one on the right is a carbide-tipped bit with a ball-bearing pilot. It can cost 3 to 4 times that of the high-speed-steel bit.*

Illus. 2-11. *Once you have gained some experience with the router, you may want to consider this second set of bits.*

sive just a few years ago, but today you can buy one for a very reasonable price. Illus. 2-19 and 2-20 show other bits that may prove useful as you gain more experience.

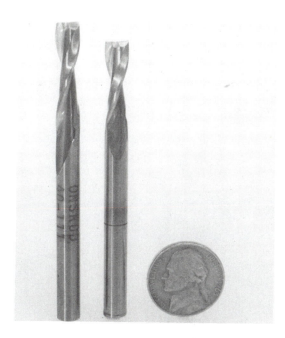

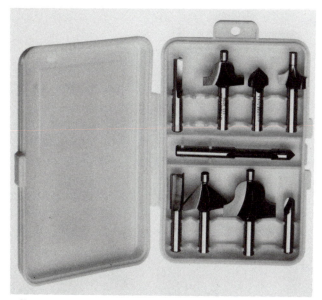

Illus. 2-12. *Sometimes manufacturers offer a variety of bits in sets for a good price, but before buying the set make sure that you want all the bits offered.*

Illus. 2-13. *You should eventually add one good spiral bit to your collection. Spiral bits cut cleanly and pull the chips out of the cut. The chips are therefore not continually re-cut, creating friction and heat. Heat and friction reduce edge sharpness.*

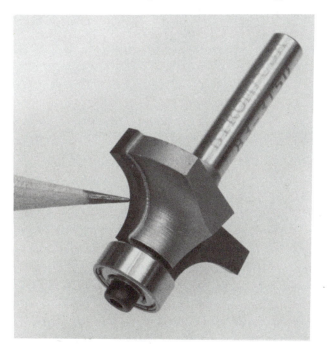

Illus. 2-14. *Quality carbide-tipped bits have high-grade carbide. This carbide is fairly thick, so the bit can be resharpened many times.*

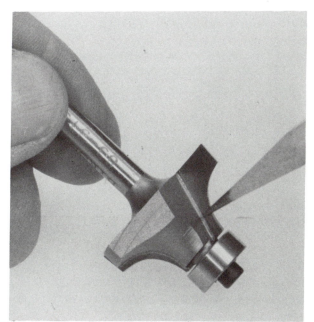

Illus. 2-15. *Always inspect the weld (or brazing) carefully before buying bits. Do not buy those bits that show irregularities and voids in their brazes. The braze on the cutting face should be smooth to effect good chip removal.*

Illus. 2-16. *Also inspect the back of the brazing.*

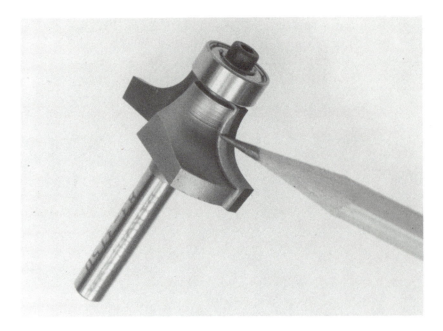

Illus. 2-17. *All these straight-cutting, carbide-tipped bits have ball-bearing "pilots."*

Illus. 2-18. *These safety bits are expensive, but are particularly recommended for beginners. They have added material behind their cutting edges. This material helps control the depth of cut of each edge at each revolution to a limit of 3/64 inch. This means that the bit cannot be abruptly pulled into the work. These bits are sold by Byrom International Corporation, Chardon, Ohio.*

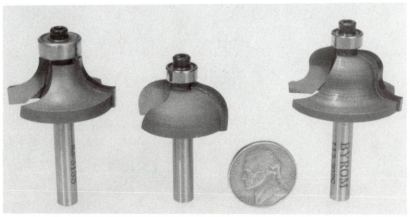

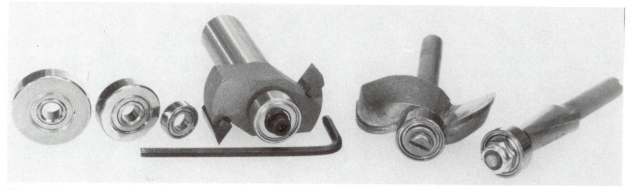

Illus. 2-19. *You can often change the cutting profiles of some bits by replacing the ball-bearing pilot with* one of a different diameter. *This means that you can use a single bit to make different cuts.*

Specialty Bits

Specialty bits are designed to cut specific materials or shapes. As a beginner, you will have very little use for these bits. Illus. 2-20, however, does show some specialty bits you'll develop an interest in later on.

Care and Maintenance

You will find yourself making a considerable investment in router bits. In fact, they may eventually cost more than your router.

To get the best and most extended use out of your bits, you'll have to have them occasionally sharpened by professionals. Either ask the person you buy your bits from where to get them sharpened, or check your Yellow Pages.

There are, however, certain things you can do to improve and extend the service life of a bit. They are as follow:

1. Keep the bits clean.

2. Store the bits properly so that their edges do not get nicked. (See Illus. 2-21.)

3. Keep all the surfaces of the bits lightly oiled so that they don't rust. (Illus. 2-22.) This is espe-

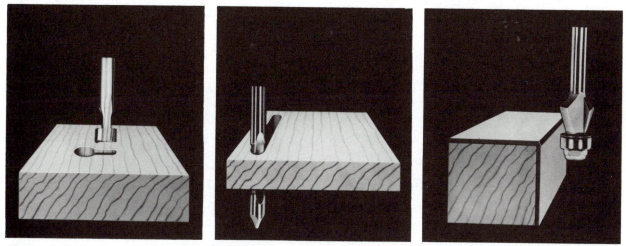

Illus. 2-20. *You may want to eventually add these three specialty bits to your collection. The bit at the far left is a keyhole bit. It is used to make hanging slots in the backs of picture frames, mirrors, shelves, cabinets, etc. The panel pilot bit shown in* the middle drills its own hole, and its pilot will follow templates and patterns. The bevel laminate trim bit on the right is used to smooth and bevel edges of plastic laminate cabinet surfaces. (A bevel is an incline or slant.)

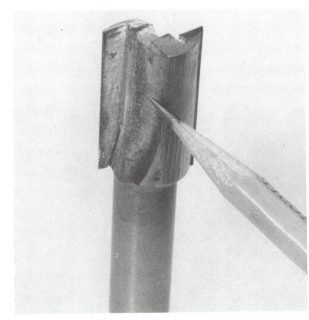

Illus. 2-21. *To make sure that the cutting edges of the bits do not become nicked, store the bits either in the convenient protective pouches they come in, or in a holder you can make yourself, as shown here.*

Illus. 2-22. *Some bit-maintenance supplies. Oven cleaners can remove the worst resin, pitch, and dirt buildup. Lubricants, such as the oil or wax spray coating shown at far right, prevent rusting and minimize resin accumulation. It is claimed that some spray lubricants, when applied to bits, reduce friction. This lowers the cutting temperature of the bit and reduces premature dulling.*

Illus. 2-23. *Resin and pitch are sticky substances that are secreted by the wood. They can build up quickly on bits. When they do, this causes the cutting edge of a bit to heat up and burn. This burning, in turn, hardens the pitch and resin, and affects the quality of the cut. To prevent this, frequently clean and lubricate the bit.*

Illus. 2-24. *Oven cleaners remove resin or pitch swiftly and efficiently. They clean right to the metal. Oven cleaners are available in gel or spray types. Both work wonderfully.*

cially important in places that are very humid. A spray oven cleaner can remove resin, pitch, and other material from the filthiest bit very quickly and efficiently. (See Illus. 2-23 and 2-24).

There are times when you will find it more convenient to "touch up" (sharpen slightly) the bit yourself. In fact, you may have to do this to some brand-new bits to get them to perform better. A small diamond hone is an ideal purchase for this, because you can use it to put beautiful edges on both carbide and high-speed-steel bits. (See Illus. 2-25–2-27).

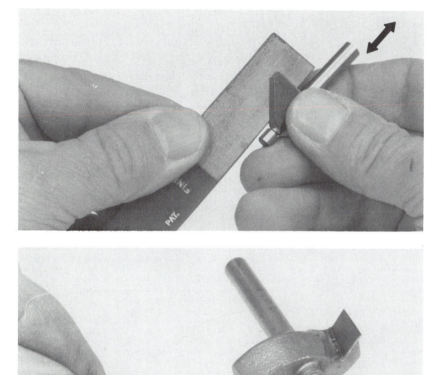

Illus. 2-25. This high-speed-steel bit is being sharpened on a flat, abrasive diamond hone. Work only the cutting face—the surface towards the flute. Do not sharpen the bevel behind the cutting edge. Also, do not let the pilot touch the abrasive.

Illus. 2-26. If the ball-bearing pilots on bits become jammed, you should remove, clean and lubricate them. If they have become damaged or worn out, replace them with new ones.

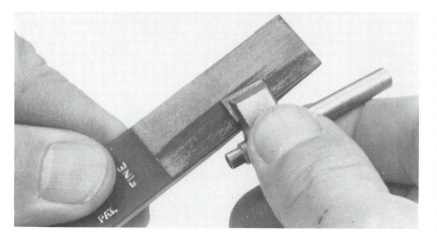

Illus. 2-27. A diamond hone will put a sharp edge and smooth face on a carbide bit quickly. Try to sharpen each cutting face the same as the others, to maintain bit balance. You have an unbalanced or bent bit if you feel any vibration through the handles of the router when you try to use the bit. In such a case, send the bit to a professional immediately. Do not use it. Note: In this photo, the ball bearing has been removed so that the bit can be honed.

Bit-Selection Guidelines

There is an amazing range of bits to choose from. This should be considered an advantage rather than a drawback, because this variety of bits allows you to pick the one best suited for the job you have in mind. If you follow the advice given below, you will find yourself with a collection of bits that will cover all your basic needs.

1. When possible, use a bit that has the shortest possible cutting-edge length and the largest cutting diameter.

2. In general, use very sharp high-speed-steel bits to rout all soft woods and hard woods. The sharper cutting edges on these bits will stay sharp longer than those on carbide bits when you are cutting solid woods.

3. Use carbide bits on solid woods only when very-long-edge sharpness is more important than the quality of the cut surface.

4. Use carbide bits for plywoods and other man-made sheet materials that contain bit-dulling glues and resins.

5. Use carbide bits when slow feed rates are necessary (such as in most freehand work, making deep slots, and sign carving) and where steady feed is interrupted with frequent hesitations, starts, and stops.

6. Use spiral bits for deep plunge-entry cuts, for deep grooving or slotting cuts, and for the smoothest trimming jobs.

Chapter 3

SAFETY TECHNIQUES

Whenever you are using a router, your personal safety should be of utmost concern. A safety-conscious attitude has to be developed. Beginners concentrate so hard on doing the job in front of them that they forget to consider whether they are doing the job safely. So, before you even pick up a router, read these instructions carefully and incorporate them into your working routine.

If you prepare properly, you can prevent accidents. This can be accomplished by thinking every operation through beforehand, no matter how simple you think it is. Visualize how you will make the cuts with the router. Ask yourself the following questions: Is the operation dangerous? Is everything clamped properly? Am I going to cut in the proper feed direction? Can I reach the switch quickly if I have to? How will I start and end the cuts? Where do I need and not need to put pressure on the router?

Do not begin the cutting operation until you are sure of the answers to these questions and any other questions you may have.

Thinking everything through beforehand helps to prevent many mishaps. Dressing properly ensures that you are adequately protected in case a mishap does occur. Incorporate the following dress guidelines into your working routine:

1. Always wear eye protection. (See Illus. 3-1.) This is especially important when you turn the power on.

2. Any time you spend more than a few minutes routing, wear hearing protection. (See Illus. 3-2.)

3. Always wear a dust mask, even if you don't have problems with dust. Fine microsized dust particles can be hazardous. (See Illus. 3-3.)

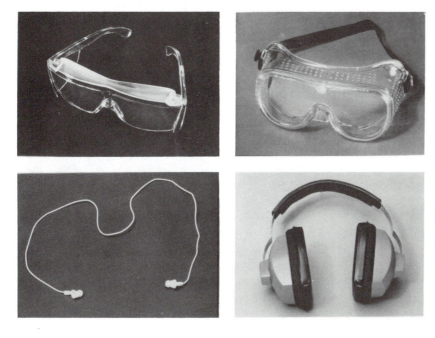

Illus. 3-1. *The protective spectacles shown on the left fit over eyeglasses, but are not recommended for heavy workshop use. The safety goggles shown on the right are better to use. They, too, fit over eyeglasses and give maximum protection.*

Illus. 3-2. *The earplugs shown on the left are satisfactory and comfortable, but are not recommended for continuous, long-term routing. The hearing protectors shown on the right are best for the severe noise levels of routers.*

Illus. 3-3. *Filtered dust masks and replacement filters offer good protection, not only from dust but also from paint spray and pollen. The type of dust mask shown here can be worn with goggles and hearing protection.*

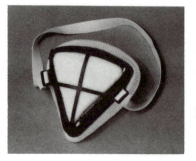

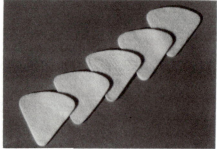

4. Make sure that loose clothing and long hair are tucked safely away. (See Illus. 3-4.)

Carefully read the following safety checklist. Many of the precautions on the list are explored in depth in Chapter 5. Follow all these precautions carefully. Remember, the router is a power tool, and all power tolls should be respected.

1. Read the owner's manual completely.

2. Make sure that the switch is off before touching the router or plugging it in.

3. Always unplug the router when changing bits and bases, or attaching and adjusting accessories, or servicing the router.

4. Make sure that the bits are clean, sharp, properly installed, and firmly tightened in the collet. This is discussed in Chapter 4.

5. Always clamp the workpiece securely to a bench or table. (See Illus. 3-4.)

6. Make multiple passes at shallower depths rather than just one deep pass. (See Illus. 3-5–3-9.)

7. Avoid routing stock of small sizes.

8. Make a test cut on scrap of a suitable size.

9. Do not use electric tools near flammable liquids or in gaseous or explosive atmospheres. They may spark.

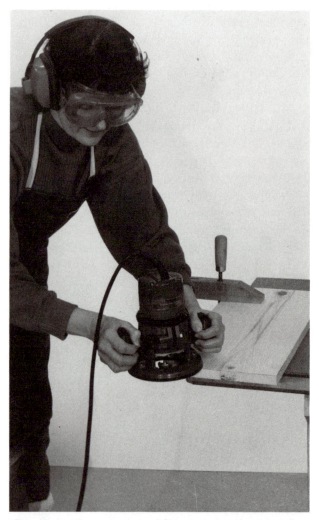

Illus. 3-4. *This person is following the proper safety guidelines. Note the eye and hearing protection, the work apron, and that there is no loose clothing, hair or jewelry. The work area is clean, and the workpiece is securely clamped to a workbench. Both hands are gripping the router, and the person's attention is focused on starting the cut.*

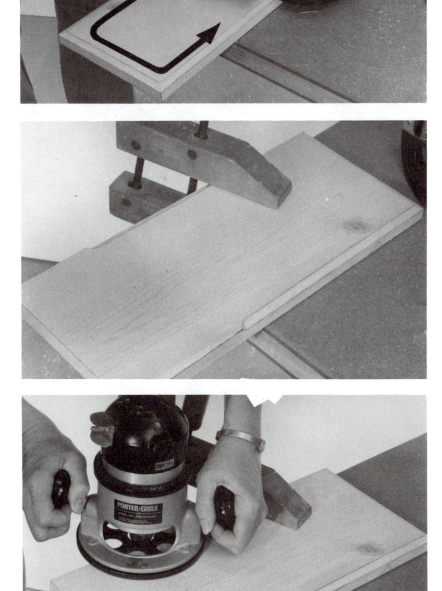

Illus. 3-5. *Make the first pass at a shallow depth. Note that the router is being fed into the work in a counterclockwise direction. Also note that the cut has been stopped here so that the work-piece can be reset under the clamp. After the workpiece has been reclamped, the cut will continue all around the board.*

Illus. 3-6. *With the first pass partially completed, turn the work-piece end for end and reclamp it to the table, as shown here.*

Illus. 3-7. *After repositioning the workpiece under the clamp, complete the first, shallow cut around all four edges of the board.*

Illus. 3-8. *Make the second pass around all four edges of the board in the same manner, but with the bit set to cut deeper.*

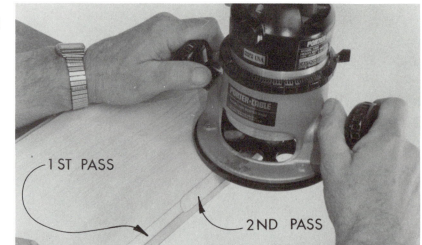

Illus. 3-9. *Depending upon the hardness of the material, the horsepower of the router, and the amount of material to be cut away, anywhere from one to four or more successively deeper passes may be required.*

10. Don't use tools in damp or wet locations.

11. Stay alert. Do not use any electric tools when tired, ill, upset, or under medication.

12. Feed the router in the proper direction: against the bit's rotation. See pages 48 and 49.

13. Make sure that you are thoroughly familiar with the router before attempting any type of cut.

14. Never start up the router with the bit in contact with the wood. Make sure that the bit will rotate freely, well away from the work, before turning on the power.

15. Make sure that you have the right kind of bit for the kind of material to be cut.

16. Never touch a bit immediately after use—it may be extremely hot.

17. Inspect the bit and collet frequently.

18. Do not use bits that are too big for your router. (See Illus. 3-10.)

19. If the switch on your router is located where you are required to reach for it or remove your grip from the router handle or knob, use a foot-switch accessory. (See Illus. 3-11 and 3-12.)

20. When possible, use a dust-collection system that will gather all the dust generated by a router. (See Illus. 3-13.)

21. Store tools not being used in a safe and dry place that is locked.

Illus. 3-10. *Beginners should not even consider buying or using large, oversized bits such as this one. Big bits require special routers, a lot of experience, special procedures, and extreme caution.*

Illus. 3-11 (**right**). *Note that the switch on this router is located some distance from the handle. If you were using a long bit and a shallow depth of cut, the switch might be even farther to reach.*

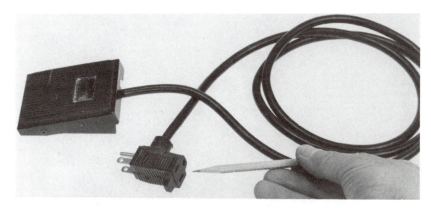

Illus. 3-12. *A foot switch is an inexpensive and convenient safety accessory which allows you to keep both hands on the router throughout each operation. The one shown here is simply an extension cord with the foot-activated switch on the end. Just plug it into an outlet and plug the router into it, as indicated in the photo.*

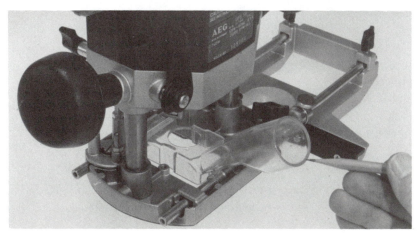

Illus. 3-13. *Another accessory that is helpful is a dust-collection piece that you can connect to the shop vacuum cleaner. This system gathers much of the dust that results when you use the router.*

Chapter 4

BASIC CUTTING GUIDELINES

The beginning router user should feel confident and in complete control of the router and workpiece the very first time he uses the tool. This can best be accomplished if he has an understanding of all the factors that can affect the quality of his work. These factors are discussed below.

Work Area and Workbench

The first requirement for using a router successfully is a clean, dry, and well-lit work area. It is essential that your workbench be sturdy, and that it provide the proper support. It's impossible to work effectively on the garage floor or on a flimsy table. Sawhorses supporting a sheet of heavy plywood will work nicely.

You can buy a portable, folding workbench with built-in, work-holding clamps. These benches are very popular and helpful. (See Illus. 4-1.) Or, you can make your own durable, workshop bench (Illus. 4-2) by using the design and plans in the next chapter. This workbench makes an ideal starting project.

Also of importance are clamps that will hold the wood pieces to be routed, and to secure fences and jigs for various table-routing jobs. (See Illus. 4-3.)

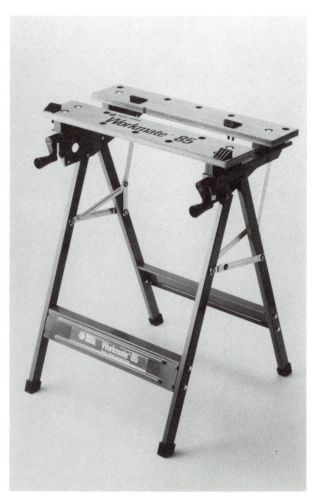

Illus. 4-1. *This popular folding workbench has built-in, work-holding clamps. It is ideal to use in a place where space is limited.*

Feed Direction The direction in which the router is moved in relation to the grain of the workpiece. Or, in router table work, the direction in which the workpiece is advanced in relation to the rotation of the bit.

Feed Rate The speed at which the router is advanced.

Moulding A wood surface shape, or a narrow strip that is principally used for decoration.

Sheet Plastic Any kind of thin plastic substance that can be either opaque or transparent, and that is used as a material for making router jigs and accessories.

Straightedge Any board or piece of sheet material with a true (straight) edge mounted to the workpiece to guide the cutting path of the router. Or, any straightedge material or tool, such as a ruler, used to check or test another line or surface for flatness or true direction.

Tempered Hardboard A low-priced sheet material made from compressed wood fibres. It is harder and more durable than its cheaper counterpart—standard hardboard.

Zeroing Out One of the steps involved when setting the depth of cut with a plunge router. It is that step in which the bit position is set and locked where the end of the bit just touches the work surface.

Table 3. *A clarification of terms that appear in this chapter.*

Illus. 4-2. *This sturdy workbench is ideal for routing and general woodworking. It is two feet wide and four feet long, and is made of 2 × 4's (pieces of wood that are 1½ and 3½ inches). Plans and instructions for making this workbench are given in the next chapter.*

Illus. 4-3. *You need a few good clamps to secure the workpiece to the bench and to hold various jigs and fixtures.*

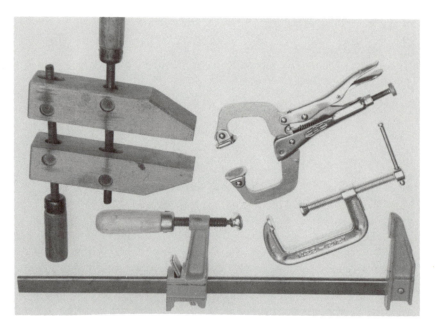

Knowing How Your Router Works

Before you even plug in the router or install a bit, you should be familiar with how the router feels and how to make all adjustments to it. With the power off, grip the router and get the feel of it. (See Illus. 4-4.) Then try different cutting motions and experiment with the adjustments until you have a complete understanding of how they work.

If it's a plunging router, move it up and down and familiarize yourself with the way it feels and with the way the lock works. Determine if it takes an upward or downward motion on the lock lever to release the router. (See Illus. 4-5.)

After you've practised handling the router with the power off, you're ready to use it with the power on. But even now, do not install a bit. Instead, follow these step-by-step procedures:

1. Make sure that you are dressed properly with goggles and hearing protection.

Illus. 4-4. *With the router unplugged from the power source and without a bit installed, become thoroughly acquainted and comfortable with all of the router's parts, clamps, and adjustments. Simulate cutting passes. Practise how to plunge and retract the router. Also, practise switching the router at the start and at the end of each pass. Lift and move the router from its resting position to the work, and back again. Always be aware of where the cord is.*

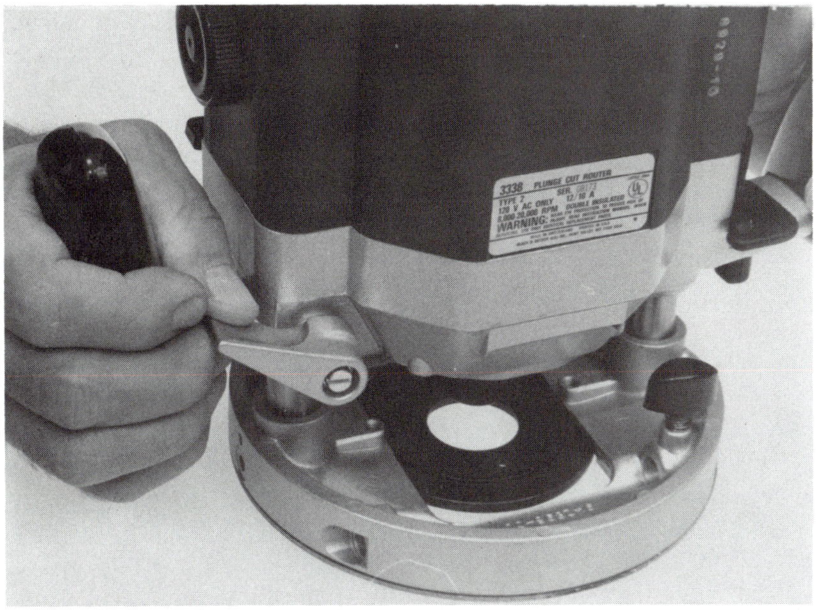

Illus. 4-5. *Practise until you have total confidence in your plunge-clamping and release abilities. Practise these skills at various motor heights, from low to high. With some practice, you will be able to retract the bit from the work instantly at any time.*

Illus. 4-6. *It is important that you know how to set the router down after using it. You can use one or two hands to set it down, as long as you're in control. Place a fixed-base router on its side, well onto the workbench. The bit should face away from you.*

2. Make sure that the switch is off before plugging in the router.

3. Grip the router firmly, as shown in Illus. 4-4, and turn on the power. Be prepared to resist the torque caused by the quick start of the motor. Get used to the noise the router makes and its thrusting power before doing anything else.

4. Now, handle the router. Move and lift it, and simulate cutting runs. Switch the router on and off for each trial pass. (See Illus. 4-6.)

Installing Bits

Follow these step-by-step procedures when installing bits:

1. Unplug the power cord!

2. If a bit is in the router, remove it first. (See Illus. 4-7 and 4-8.)

3. To install a new bit, insert the bit completely into the bottom of the collet and then

draw it back about ⅟16 inch before tightening the collet with the wrench provided with the router. (See Illus. 4-9 and 4-10.)

On some routers, it is possible to remove the motor unit from the base to change the bits. If this can be done, do it.

4. Inspect the collet. If dust has accumulated, wipe it off. If there is pitch, soak it off with a cleaner. If the bit you are adding sticks inside the collet, gently tap on the collet nut with a stick. Do not use pliers on the bit or strike the bit to free it.

Illus. 4-7. *One technique for loosening the collet nut. The nut should be rotated counterclockwise (against the direction that the hands on a clock move). Note the operator's open hand.*

Illus. 4-8. *The operator can loosen the bit on this router by turning it with just one wrench and pushing down on the push-button spindle lock.*

Illus. 4-9. *The easiest way to tighten the collet is to use the surface of the workbench for leverage, and an open hand, as shown, to prevent bruised fingers. Turn the nut clockwise (in the direction that the hands of a clock move) to tighten it.*

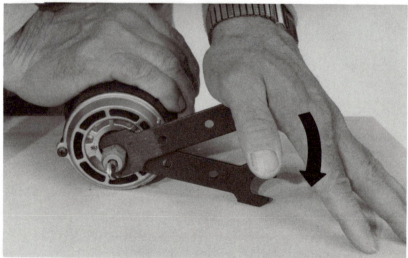

Illus. 4-10. *This collet is being tightened with one hand. Use this method for routers that stand on their motor ends, and for plunge routers on which two wrenches have to be used. Note: Exchanging the position of the two wrenches, as shown, loosens the collet nut.*

Illus. 4-11. *Here the operator is changing a bit on a plunge router that has a spindle lock. Do not strike the posts with the wrench.*

Setting the Depth of Cut

The amount of bit protruding below the base is called the depth of cut. Sometimes you will find that the cut is too deep to make in one pass. In such cases, you will have reset the depth of cut.

It is easy to set the depth of cut on a fixed-based router. (See Illus. 4-12 and 4-13.)

You can also quickly and conveniently set the depth of cut on a plunge router, especially when

Illus. 4-12 (right). *It is easy to set the depth of cut on a fixed-base router. The amount of exposed bit is the depth of cut.*

Illus. 4-13. *This non-essential aid—called a depth-of-cut gauge—helps determine depth-of-cut settings.*

the cut to be made is a deep one and is best made in several passes. Check your operator's manual for the exact procedure, because all plunge routers have slightly different mechanisms. Generally, however, it is done as follows:

1. Loosen the stop pole so that it slides down and is in contact with the stop block. (See Illus. 4-14.)

2. At the same time, lower the motor unit until the bit just comes into contact with the workpiece. (See Illus. 4-15.)

3. Lock the clamp lever to hold the router body in this position.

4. Raise the stop pole to the appropriate height and lock it securely. The total depth of cut equals the space between the bottom of the stop pole and the stop. (See Illus. 4-16.)

5. Release the motor clamp. (See Illus. 4-17.) The bit will now be able to plunge lower and to enter the wood.

On most plunge routers, deep cuts can be pre-set for two or three passes with the aid of rotating stop blocks. (See Illus. 4-18–4-20.) A new stop is rotated into position after each pass. This increases the depth each time. Check your manual to determine exactly how to do it.

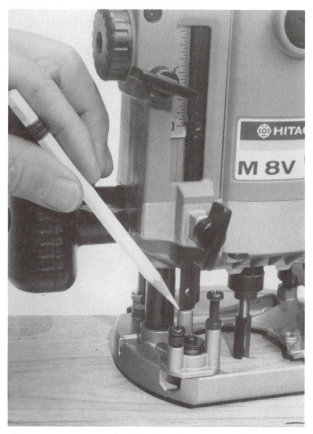

Illus. 4-14. *To set the depth of cut on a plunging router, first loosen the stop pole and let it down so that it touches the stop.*

Illus. 4-15. *At the same time, lower the motor unit until the bit just touches the work surface; then lock the clamp lever. This is known as "zeroing out" the router.*

Illus. 4-16. *Raise the stop pole the appropriate distance. This distance will equal the total depth of cut desired. Clamp the stop pole tightly. The space between the stop and the bottom of the stop pole equals the depth of cut.*

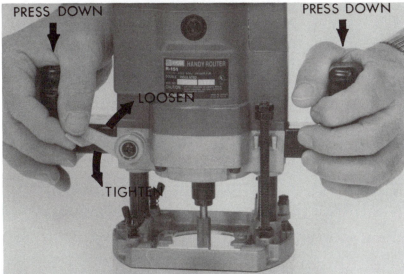

Illus. 4-17. *When you release the motor clamp, the bit will plunge. This allows you to lower it into the work.*

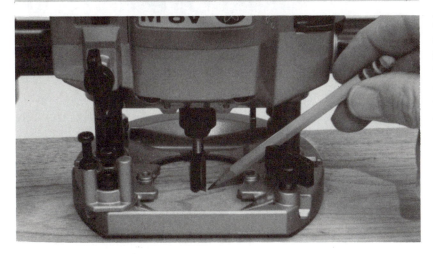

Illus. 4-18. *The first step in setting a plunge router for one or multiple depths of cut is to "zero out" the router—that is, to bring the bit down so that it lightly touches the surface of the wood. Then clamp the motor at this position.*

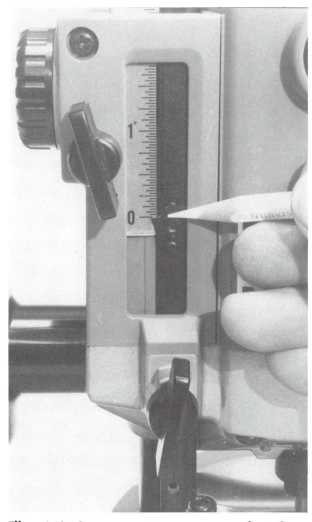

Illus. 4-19. *On some routers, you can readjust the scale to a zero cutting depth. This will make it easier for you to set the depth stopper pole.*

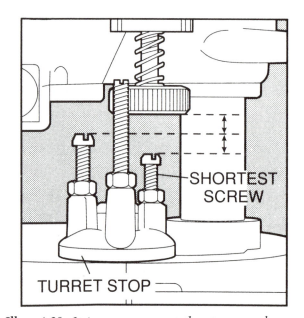

Illus. 4-20. *It is easy to preset the stops on plunge routers for multiple passes at predetermined depths. Here the shortest and second-shortest screw stops will be used for two passes. The third screw (stop) is used to make deeper cuts in three passes.*

2. Start with a shallow depth setting and prepare to make your first edge-forming cut. (See Illus. 4-22.)

3. Rout as far as possible, and then reset the work under the clamp as necessary to complete the cut. (Refer to Illus. 3-5–3-8, pages 37 and 38.)

Practice Cuts

Now it is time to test the cutting ability of the router on scraps of wood. Make sure that your practice cuts are on scraps that are long and wide enough to handle safely. Follow these procedures:

1. Clamp the workpiece to the workbench. For edge-forming jobs that go all around the board, you usually clamp the work so that one end and most of one edge extend over the edge of the workbench. (See Illus. 4-21.)

Feed Direction and Feed Rates

Feed direction and feed rates are important factors in safe and effective routing. As a rule, *always feed against the rotation of the bit.* (See Illus. 4-23.)

You should be aware that whenever you are doing edge-forming operations, less than half of the router is actually supported on the work itself. When you are routing around a square corner, less than a quarter of the base area is supported on the work.

Illus. 4-21. *Clamp the workpiece to the bench. When you are going to edge-form a piece, place it so that an end and edge of the board extend beyond the edge of the workbench.*

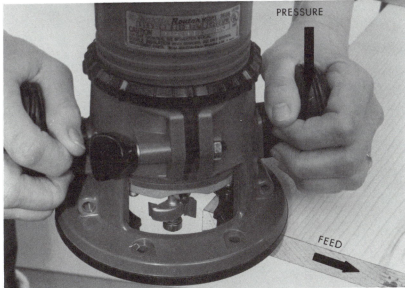

Illus. 4-22. *Be certain that the bit is not in contact with the workpiece when you start the router up. Turn on the power, hold the base flat on the surface, and advance the router and bit into the workpiece in a left-to-right feed direction, against the rotation of the bit. Note here that less than ¼ of the base is actually on the surface. Here the operator must also provide sufficient downward pressure with his left hand to keep the router from tipping.*

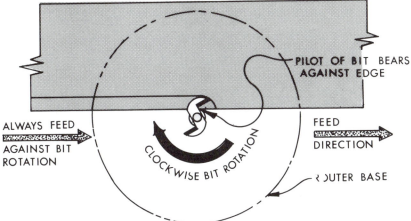

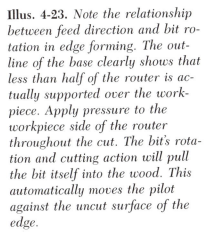

Illus. 4-23. *Note the relationship between feed direction and bit rotation in edge forming. The outline of the base clearly shows that less than half of the router is actually supported over the workpiece. Apply pressure to the workpiece side of the router throughout the cut. The bit's rotation and cutting action will pull the bit itself into the wood. This automatically moves the pilot against the uncut surface of the edge.*

The ideal feed rate is determined by many factors. These factors include the size and sharpness of the bit, the depth of cut, the hardness of the material being cut, grain direction, horsepower, and speed (revolutions per minute, or rpm). By following these general rules, you will be able to determine the ideal feed direction. A fairly fast feed rate is better than too slow a feed rate. If the feed rate is fairly fast, the bit will not burn. Too slow a feed will burn the wood under solid pilots as well as under the cutting edges. (See Illus. 4-24 and 4-25.) The best way to determine if you are feeding the bit into the workpiece properly is through sound and feel. This you'll learn through experience. You'll soon realize when a router is overloaded, bits are dull, you are force-feeding the bit, or the bit is becoming overheated.

Illus. 4-24. *This hard maple was routed with a light-duty router. The final ogee cut at right was made in four successive passes at increasing depths, as shown. A high-speed-steel bit with a solid pilot was used.*

Illus. 4-25. *This hard oak shows burns that were caused by hesitations in the rate at which the router was fed. A uniform, uninterrupted feed rate will eliminate these markings, which are almost impossible to sand out.*

Illus. 4-26. To make narrow mouldings, first edge-rout a wider board and then rip off the moulding strip.

Edge-forming Technique

There are some factors you should be aware of when edge-forming. (Edge-forming is routing along the edge and/or end of the board.) They are:

1. The depth of cut is actually made from two directions: vertically and horizontally.

2. Do not force the solid pilot of the bit hard against the edge of the piece when feeding the bit. Use a slight side pressure to counteract the natural pull of the bit into the work. This will minimize burning and charring under the pilot.

3. Make a final pass at a shallow depth with a smooth, uninterrupted feed, and with the pilot riding fully but "lightly" on the edge.

4. You can make narrow mouldings safely by edge-forming wider boards and then ripping the moulding strip off, as shown in Illus. 4-26.

Straight-Line Surface Routing

Because the bits used for surface routing do not have pilots that will control the direction of the router, some sort of guiding device is needed.

Two basic guiding devices used are: (1) An *edge-guide* router accessory, and (2) a *straightedge* of a suitable length of available lumber.

The edge-guide accessory can be bought wherever you would buy your router. It is adjustable, and clamps to the base of your router. It rides the edge of the workpiece and guides the router so

Illus. 4-27. An edge-guide accessory attached to the base of the router, as shown here, makes straight-line surface routing easy. It does require a little practice to get used to routing with an edge-guide accessory, especially at the beginning of the cut and at its completion, when only one-half of the guide fence is actually on the edge of the board.

that the bit will make a cut parallel to the guiding edge. (See Illus. 4-27.)

Any simple board or strip of wood with one straight and true edge makes a good straight-line routing guide. Once you have one, keep it close by. Consider it almost like a helpful tool. Use it when a commercial edge-guide is not available or is not long enough for the job. You can also use a straightedge when the direction of cut is angular or not parallel to the edge of the workpiece.

When using a straightedge to make a surface cut, place it in its proper position so that the desired cut can be made with the router base riding against it. This is shown in Illus. 4-28. Clamp or tack the straightedge to the workpiece. It must be placed exactly parallel to the line of cut and at a distance equal to the measurement from the cutting edge of the bit to the outside edge of the router base. You must feed the router against the rotation of the bit so that the thrust of the router (from the cutting action of the bit)

pulls the router towards the straightedge. Do not feed in the direction of the rotation of the bit because the router will tend to pull itself away from the straightedge.

Auxiliary Sub-Bases

Sooner or later, you'll find it advantageous to replace the sub-base on your router with a special one that you have made yourself or wish to purchase. Since router sub-bases have central openings that come in different sizes, you may want to make one that has an opening larger or smaller than the one on the sub-base that came with the router. (See Illus. 4-29 and 4-30.)

You can make your own bases from hard material such as tempered hardboard, ¼-inch-thick plywood, or sheet plastic. Use the existing base as a pattern and drill mounting holes to match.

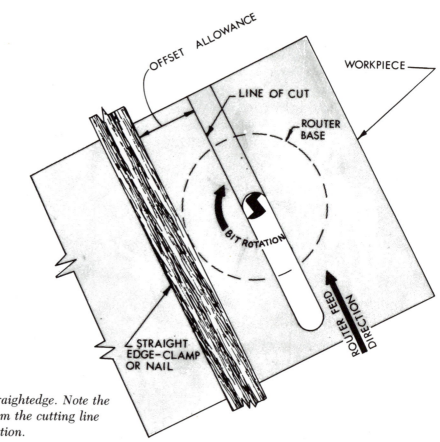

Illus. 4-28. Routing against a straightedge. Note the amount of space that's off-set from the cutting line and the recommended feed direction.

Illus. 4-29. *The two bases shown on the right were made in the workshop. (One of these bases is shown attached to the router.) The base on the left was the pattern for these two bases. Note the horseshoe shape of the base attached to the router. It is designed to give additional visibility to the line of cut when the operator is making freehand routing designs on the surface of the wood. The base with the small holes was designed for routing the ends of narrow boards. It provides better support than one with a large hole in many edge-forming jobs.*

Illus. 4-30. *Many router users like transparent bases. In fact, I often make one myself. The clear-plastic one shown on the right can be purchased from a manufacturer as an accessory.*

You may have a router with a nonremovable sub-base that is permanently glued on. In such a case, attach the auxiliary base over the existing sub-base with double-faced tape. Make sure that it is on securely; you do not want it to come loose during an operation.

Chapter 5

MAKING A WORKBENCH

I have learned through years of experience in the workshop that the best way to teach a beginner essential joinery cuts and other techniques is to provide him with a project to work on, and to give him the proper guidance. A workbench project (Illus. 5-1–5-3) provides an excellent opportunity for you to practise some basic and essential routing skills that involve the use of the popular edge-guide accessory. You can also apply these skills to other projects.

This workbench can be made at minimum expense from readily available, inexpensive construction-type wood. In making it, you'll learn how to lay out the material and rout grooves and mortises and tenons. The mortise-and-tenon joint is one of the most popular and strongest joints in woodworking. You'll also learn how to overcome any design limitations the router may have in order to complete the project safely and easily.

The router used to build this workbench is a ¼-inch plunge router that has 1 horsepower. This router has an adjustable straight-cutting-guide attachment (commonly called an edge guide). This edge guide attaches to the router base. (See Illus. 5-4 and 5-5.) It's recommended that you screw an additional wooden fence to it, as shown in the photos. This fence should be of sufficient length to provide more surface that can be placed against the edge of the workpiece, and thus it makes it easier for you to feed the router.

Illus. 5-1. *This workbench, 2 feet wide and 4 feet long, is easy and inexpensive to make. Though this one has a purchased top, you can use a piece of plywood ¾ inch thick × 24 inches wide × 48 inches long to make a fine top.*

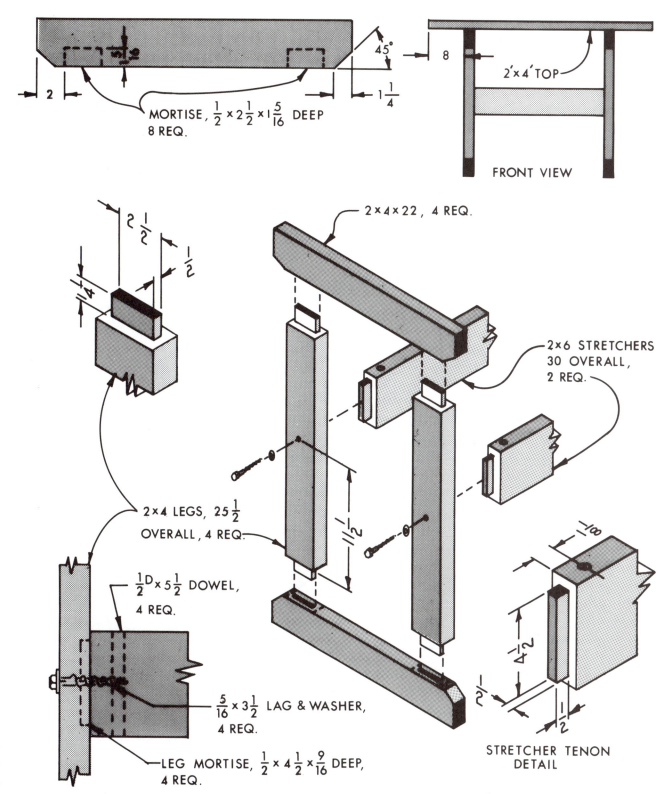

45°

8

2′ × 4′ TOP

FRONT VIEW

2

MORTISE, $\frac{1}{2}$ × $2\frac{1}{2}$ × $1\frac{5}{16}$ DEEP
8 REQ.

$1\frac{1}{4}$

$2\frac{1}{2}$

$\frac{1}{2}$

$\frac{1}{4}$

2 × 4 × 22, 4 REQ.

2 × 6 STRETCHERS
30 OVERALL,
2 REQ.

2 × 4 LEGS, $25\frac{1}{2}$
OVERALL, 4 REQ.

$1\frac{1}{2}$

$\frac{1}{2}$D × $5\frac{1}{2}$ DOWEL,
4 REQ.

$\frac{5}{16}$ × $3\frac{1}{2}$ LAG & WASHER,
4 REQ.

LEG MORTISE, $\frac{1}{2}$ × $4\frac{1}{2}$ × $\frac{9}{16}$ DEEP,
4 REQ.

$\frac{1}{8}$

$4\frac{1}{2}$

$\frac{1}{2}$

$\frac{1}{2}$

STRETCHER TENON
DETAIL

Illus. 5-2. *Here are the construction details for the workbench. Remember that when you buy a 2 × 4 from a lumberyard it actually measures 1½ inches thick × 3½ inches wide. A 2 × 6 measures 1½ inches thick × 5½ inches wide.*

Illus. 5-3. *All of the pieces for the base shown here can be cut from the following three pieces of construction-grade lumber: one is 2 inches thick × 4 inches wide × 8 feet long, one 2 inches thick × 4 inches wide × 10 feet long, and one 2 inches thick × 6 inches wide × 6 feet long. The lengths for these pieces take into account extra space for test cuts.*

Illus. 5-4. *A straight-cutting edge guide is attached to the base of this plunging router. You can improve the function of the guide for certain cuts by attaching a narrow wood strip to lengthen the fence surface. This wood strip guides along the edge of the workpiece.*

Illus. 5-5. *With the strip of wood attached to the fence, it is also easier to measure to make setup adjustments.*

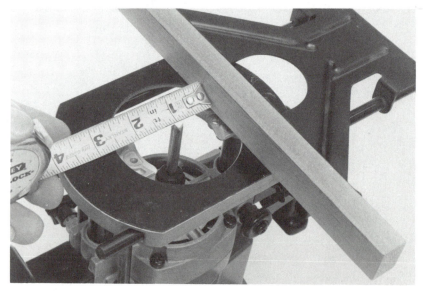

Illus. 5-6–5-25 take you step by step through all of the important procedures involved in making the strong supporting substructure of the workbench. The bench shown in the illustrations has a ready-made, purchased top that measures 1¾ inches thick × 2 feet wide × 4 feet long. However, you can make your own 1½-inch-thick top from a half sheet of ¾-inch-thick plywood that's either 4 feet wide × 4 feet long or 2 feet wide × 8 feet long or any other combination of multiple layers of various sheet materials. Just one piece of ⅝- or ¾-inch-thick plywood top that's 2 feet wide × 4 feet long will also serve almost all routing needs. If you want a longer bench, simply lengthen the dimensions of the stretchers shown in Illus. 5-2 as desired.

I designed this workbench so that the top on each end overhangs 8 inches, and provides ample space for clamps to grip workpieces on one end and for a vise to be added to the other end. Also, the strong stretchers will provide good support for an optional shelf that can hold very heavy objects like cans of paint or lumber.

Once all the pieces have been machined, glue the four pieces together comprising the vertical leg end assemblies first. (See Illus. 5-22.) Complete the assembly by gluing and bolting the stretchers to the legs. (See Illus. 5-23–5-25.) Make or buy your top, and fasten it to the substructure. The workbench is complete.

Illus. 5-6. *You can trim rough-sawn 2 × 4's to their precise finished lengths with your router, as shown here. Make one cut from each side with the bit set to slightly more than half of the thickness (about ¹³⁄₁₆ inch). (See Illus. 5-7.)*

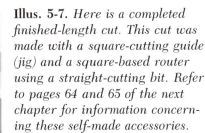

Illus. 5-7. *Here is a completed finished-length cut. This cut was made with a square-cutting guide (jig) and a square-based router using a straight-cutting bit. Refer to pages 64 and 65 of the next chapter for information concerning these self-made accessories.*

Illus. 5-8. *Next, lay out only one mortise 2 inches from the end of one of the foot or top cross members, as shown on the piece on the right. Only the length of the mortise, as shown at the left, needs to be transferred to each piece. There will be eight identical mortises to rout out.*

Illus. 5-9. *"Zero-out" the router and set the cutting depth at 1⁵⁄₁₆ inches. Plan to use the multiple depth stops because a cut of this depth should be made in multiple passes—at least six, and preferably eight, depending upon the size and style of bit available.*

Illus. 5-10. *You have to make some mortise cuts in multiple passes to arrive at the correct width and the correct depth of the mortise. If you have a ½-inch-diameter bit, adjust the fence of the edge guide so that the cut will be made down the center. If you have to use a narrower bit (¼, ⁵⁄₁₆, or ³⁄₈ inch), you can still make the ½-inch-wide mortise, but with extra passes at new settings. Set up the router guide so that the bit will cut the wall of the mortise that is farthest from the edge guide, as shown. This way, if you slightly tip the router or the fence is not held against the work tightly, the mortise will not be widened.*

Illus. 5-11. *The mortises will be automatically and perfectly centered if you plan to make cuts with the router guided from each side of the workpiece. Even if you use a ½-inch bit and make the mortise slightly oversize, you can cut the tenon to fit later. The two test cuts shown here were made by plunging the router to very shallow depths; one cut was made from each side of the 2 × 4. Since the test cuts are so shallow, you can still make slight adjustments and check them again before making the actual cuts.*

Illus. 5-12. *Here, the operator is cutting the first side (wall) of the mortise by making successive lengthwise passes (in this case, he is using a 5/16-inch-diameter bit); he will make these passes until the full depth of the mortise is achieved. Note the scrap or second piece clamped to the workpiece; this provides additional support for the router base when it is being used on narrow edges. Since 2 × 4's have fairly wide edges, the extra support really isn't needed. The operator will cut by working from both sides and routing to the length of the mortise, which is indicated by just the two layout lines.*

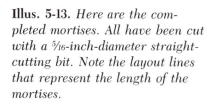

Illus. 5-13. *Here are the completed mortises. All have been cut with a 5/16-inch-diameter straight-cutting bit. Note the layout lines that represent the length of the mortises.*

Illus. 5-14. *It is easier to make wider mortises with a large diameter bit. Here a ½-inch-diameter bit is shown being used to cut the ½ inch wide × 4½ inches long × 9/16 inch deep mortises in the workbench's legs. These mortises are cut into the center of the legs, both vertically and horizontally. Thus, the legs can be assembled end for end, and the stretchers will still be the same distance from the floor.*

Illus. 5-15. *It is difficult and dangerous to accurately cut the shoulders for tenons on the ends of 2 × 4's, as shown here. Note that the router base will not have adequate support. Also, there is not enough wood bearing against the fence—just the width of the workpiece edge (See Illus. 5-16).*

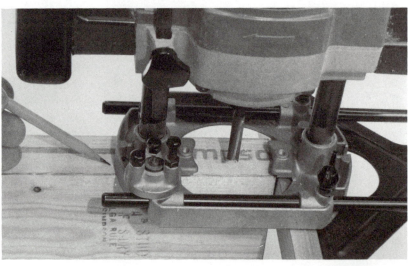

Illus. 5-16. *Here's what is likely to happen if you try to cut the shoulders for tenons in the way shown in Illus. 5-15. The router would tip. It would be virtually impossible to guide it safely, horizontally or vertically. The hole opening in the base is too large, leaving little support under it. Sometimes an auxiliary base with a small hole is helpful, but not necessarily in this case.*

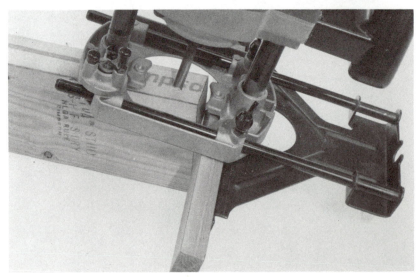

Illus. 5-17. *It's best to assemble all of the pieces so that you can make the shoulder cuts for the tenons all at once on the 2 × 4 edges. Note that only one tenon needs to be laid out. You can use this tenon to match the widest mortise you've previously cut, should any of the 2 × 4's differ in thickness and cause differences in mortise widths.*

Illus. 5-18. *The first router passes cut the shoulders for the tenons on the edges of the 2 × 4 work-bench legs.*

Illus. 5-19. *Make quick test cuts as shown on a length of scrap to check the thickness and fit of the tenon.*

Illus. 5-20. *Routing the cheeks of the tenon. Use the widest bit available to give the smoothest and flattest finished surface to the cheeks of the tenons. Note: The operator must still maintain good pressure over the left part of the base riding on the workpiece to prevent the router from tipping towards the right.*

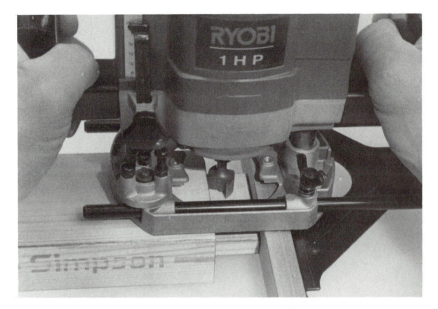

Illus. 5-21. *Rather than squaring out the corners of all the mortises to fit the tenons, it's easier and faster to round the tenons, as shown, with a knife, chisel, or file.*

Illus. 5-22. *Assemble the vertical leg members first with glue and clamps. Check the assembly for squareness, as shown.*

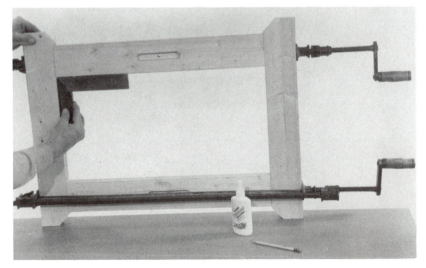

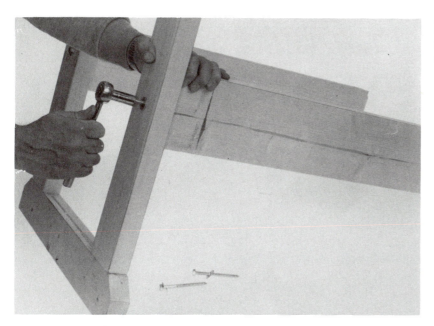

Illus. 5-23. *Fasten the stretchers to one leg assembly with lag bolts with washers.*

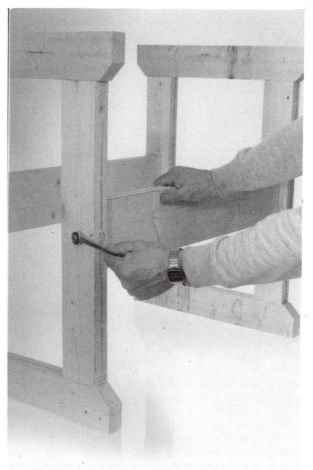

Illus. 5-24. *Bolt the stretchers to the second leg assembly. Note the mortise of the leg receiving the tenon on the end of the stretcher.*

Illus. 5-25. *Install the final lag bolt. This will complete the assembly of the substructure.*

Chapter 6

MAKING STRAIGHT AND SQUARE CUTS

A beginning woodworker may find that it is not easy to cut a board straight or square using a handsaw, even if it's a portable, electric-powered saw. He'll often find that he has cut the board too short or inaccurately in some other way. However, a router, when used with easy-to-make jigs (shop-made accessories), is able to easily and accurately make straight and square cuts.

The three jigs that are helpful in making straight and square cuts are the T-square guide, the square-trimming guide, and the auxiliary square base. Though the square base works well with the T-square guide and square-trimming guide, you do not have to use it with these two guides.

The T-square and square-trimming guides are easy to make and you'll find yourself using them often. It is better if you make both guides at the same time. (See Illus. 6-1.) First, diagonally cut one piece of ⅜- or ½-inch-thick plywood that is 12 inches wide × 14 inches long to make the straightedge parts for each jig. Then fasten wood-strip stops at right angles, as shown in Illus. 6-1. The guides are now complete.

You can use either of the guides with the standard factory sub-base that comes with your router, or you can make your own square sub-base, as shown in Illus. 6-2. You will be able to do many jobs faster and more accurately with a square base.

Make your square base from hardboard, plywood, or plastic that is about ¼ inch thick. Use the sub-base that has come with your router as a pattern for the hole-mounting locations in the sub-base you are making. Make your base the size you want, so that it will provide four differ-

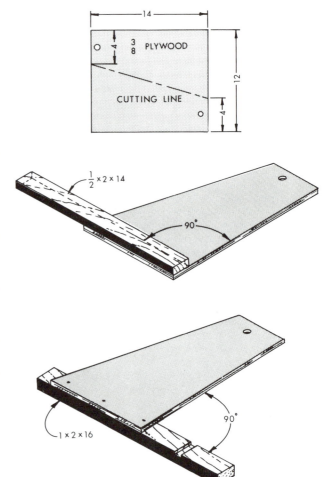

Illus. 6-1. *Shown in the middle is the square-trimming guide. Shown on the bottom is the T-square jig. The diagram at the top shows how to cut plywood to make the straightedge parts for both. As indicated by the diagram, this plywood is ⅜ inch thick, 12 inches wide, and 14 inches long. The cutting line shows where to cut the plywood to get the straightedge parts for the guides.*

Illus. 6-2. *The square base on this router makes routing fast and more accurate. A router with a square base can make any of four passes at different distances from a guiding edge without requiring any additional adjustments.*

Illus. 6-3. *The existing sub-base shown on the left provides the mounting-screw-hole pattern for the square base. Note that the center hole (and the bit) will, by design, be off-set different distances from each of the four edges.*

ent distances from each edge to the bit. (See Illus. 6-3.)

If, for example, you are using a ¼-inch-diameter bit, make the distance from one edge to the bit one that's easy to remember, such as exactly 3 inches. Make one of the two adjoining edges 3¹⁄₁₆ inches from the bit, and the remaining two edges 3⅛ and 3¼ inches from the bit. Mount the base to the router, and check its four cutting distances on scrap wood.

Your router now has the capability of making four different cuts at four different distances off-set from a guiding straightedge. The line of cut will depend upon which edge of the base is selected to guide the router.

Using the T-Square Guide

Illus. 6-4 shows how a dado can be quickly widened, using the same bit, a T-square guide, and a router with a square base. A different edge of the base is used with each successive pass of the router.

If you prefer to cut more or less material per pass, you'll have to plan and make your base accordingly. You may decide, for example, to make a very fine second trimming cut, one that's a mere ¹⁄₃₂ inch, or even ¹⁄₆₄ inch. To do this, you only have to orientate the router position and make the trimming pass rather than reset or move the straightedge or guide over this small distance.

Remember, the T-square jig should always be clamped on top of the workpiece, as shown in Illus. 6-4. Make sure that it is clamped securely and tightly against the edge of the workpiece; this will ensure that you get square cuts.

Using the Square-Trimming Guide

The square-trimming guide is used to trim and true rough-sawn cuts. (See Illus. 6-5.) Depend-

ing upon the kind of router bit or routing setup used, clamp the square-trimming jig either on top of the workpiece, as shown in Illus. 6-6, or under the workpiece, as in Illus. 6-11. When it is clamped on top, guide the edge of the router base against it. When it is clamped under the board, use a straight ball-bearing trimming bit that follows directly along the straight edge of the guide. In this latter case, the type, size, or shape of the router base is inconsequential.

Illus. 6-8 and 6-9 show how to trim and smooth a rough, hand-sawn end cut to a beautiful, precise square surface. Although spiral bits are often preferred for many deep-slotting and mortising jobs, straight-fluted bits can trim the surfaces with about the same results. (See Illus. 6-10.)

The ideal bit to use to trim work is a straight-

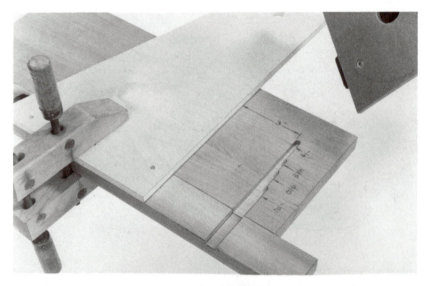

Illus. 6-4. *The T-square jig, shown clamped to the workpiece, and the router with a square base have been used to make a series of dado cuts. As shown here, you can rout dadoes with any one of four different widths without moving the T-square jig or changing the size of the bit. The off-set square base of the router makes this possible. Feeding the router into the work with a different edge on the router's square base along the T-square straightedge results in a cut made at a different distance from the T-square guide.*

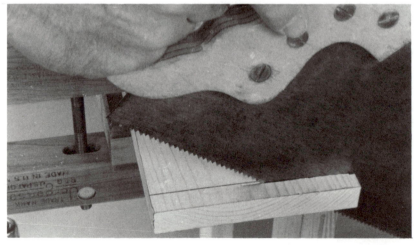

Illus. 6-5. *To use a square-trimming guide, first saw the board slightly longer than desired with a hand or power saw. This way, you can later trim the board to its precise length using the router and the square-trimming guide.*

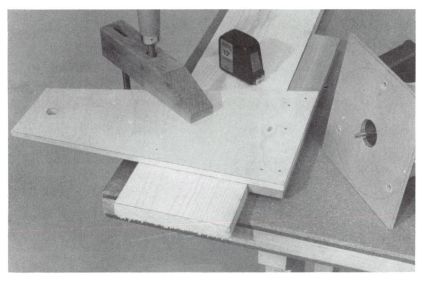

Illus. 6-6. *The workbench, workpiece, and square-trimming guide are set up so that the base of the router will follow along the straightedge. The jig must be clamped on top of the workpiece, as shown, and off-set a distance from the line of cut that equals the distance from one selected edge of the base to the cutting edge of the bit. This trimming guide can also be used to cut dadoes and grooves with or without a square-base router.*

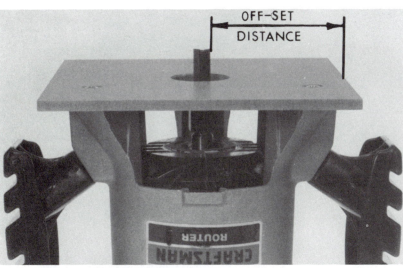

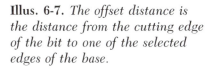

Illus. 6-7. *The offset distance is the distance from the cutting edge of the bit to one of the selected edges of the base.*

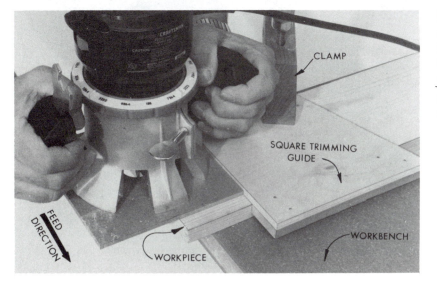

Illus. 6-8. *Using a router with a square base and a square-trimming guide. Clamp the guide the distance it should be off-set from the end of the board so that you can make the light trimming cut exactly where desired.*

Illus. 6-9. *A closeup view that shows the cutting action of the operation that was set up in Illus. 6-7. Note how smoothly the bit cleans and trims this rough, hand-sawn cut that was made on the end of a pine board.*

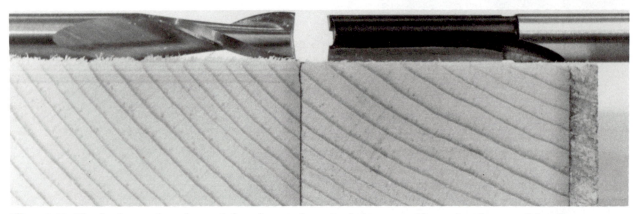

Illus. 6-10. *The high-speed-steel spiral-flute bit on the left and the straight-flute carbide-tipped bit on the right were used to make these cuts on soft wood.*

Both bits cut effectively. The spiral bit, however, leaves some fine feathering, or ragged edges, on the top surface of the board.

Illus. 6-11. *The square-trimming guide jig is set up on the work-bench to square an end of a wide, hardwood board with a router and a ball-bearing trimming bit. Note that the jig is clamped be-tween the workpiece and the workbench, and positioned so that the cut will be made beyond the edge of the workbench.*

flute trimming bit that has a ball-bearing pilot. Clamp the square-trimming guide under the workpiece, and position it so that the cut is made beyond the edge of the bench, as shown in Illus. 6-11. Illus. 6-12 and 6-13 are close-ups of the cut that show the cutting action of the bit and the resulting condition of the cut surface.

You can also use a ball-bearing-guided straight-flute bit to cut curved and irregular profiles to true and perfect shapes. In such work, a template pattern is made to guide the bit and the cut. This is known as pattern or template routing. Template or pattern routing is discussed in Chapter 10.

Illus. 6-12. Here's a view of the cutting action of the ball-bearing-guided trimming bit when it is used with the square-trimming jig. Note that the board that will be trimmed square is clamped over the jig and to the workbench table. The ball bearing guides the bit, following the straightedge of the jig, making a perfectly straight and square-trimming cut.

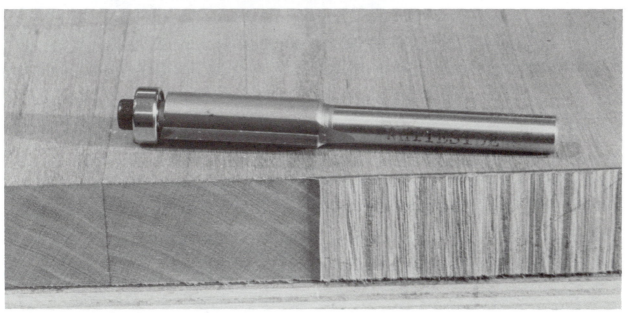

Illus. 6-13. A closeup look that shows on the left the smooth cut the trimming bit makes on end grain of this cherry hardwood. The untrimmed, rough-cut area at the right shows the surface as typically cut with a band saw or with a hand-held sabre saw. The smooth router-trimmed surface is not only straight and perfectly square—it will only need minimal sanding, if any at all.

Chapter 7

MAKING A BOOKCASE

In Chapter 5, you discovered how to make a mortise-and-tenon joint. In addition to this joint, there are a number of other joints and cuts you need to know in order to make furniture, cabinets, and accessories for your home.

As with the workbench project in Chapter 5, the best way to learn these cuts is by building a piece—in this instance, a bookcase. (See Illus. 7-1.) While building this project, you'll learn how to trim and square ends to length, make end and edge rabbets, dadoes, and grooves (or slots), trim joints, and round over or form a decorative edge.

The construction details for the bookcase are given in Illus. 7-2. Make the major parts from two pieces of 1-inch-thick × 10-inch-wide No. 2 pine boards. (This material actually measures ¾ inch in thickness and 9¼ inches in width when

you buy it.) One piece should be 8 feet long. The other piece should be 6 feet long.

If you decide to use a back panel on the bookcase, you'll need a piece of plywood approximately 25 inches long × 35 inches wide. However, you can omit the back of the bookcase entirely and use this project for basement or workshop storage.

Follow these step-by-step instructions for making the bookcase:

1. Select the best areas of the boards. Use these areas for the top piece. Then select the next-best areas for the side members.

2. Lay out and mark off all the pieces to a

Illus. 7-1. *This simple bookcase is an ideal project on which to practise joint-making methods or other cuts. It is made of inexpensive No. 2 pine, and has an adjustable shelf. Without its back panel, this project could also be used to store items in the garage or basement.*

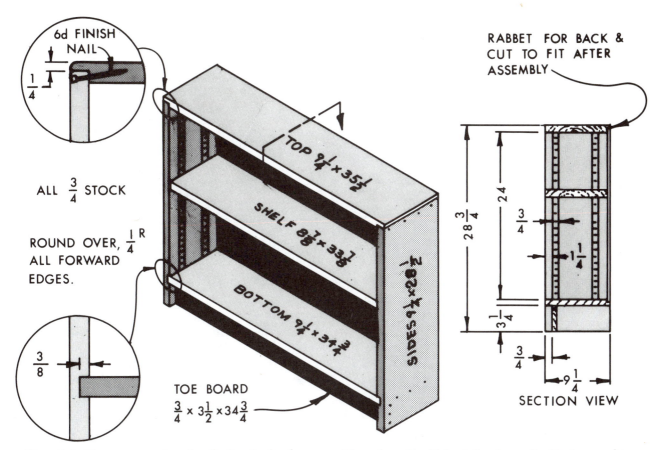

Illus. 7-2. *The construction details for the bookcase. Cut the major parts—the top, shelf, bottom and sides—from two pieces of 1-inch-thick × 10-inch-wide No. 2 pine. One piece should be 6 feet long.*

The other should be 8 feet long. You'll also need to purchase two pieces of adjustable metal shelf standards that are 4 feet in length. Cut these pieces to a length of 2 feet with a hacksaw.

rough-length dimension that is about ⅛ to ¼ inch longer than the required lengths. This will give you a little extra area for the trimming operations to square the ends. Cut the parts to their rough lengths with a hand or power saw.

3. Square the ends on the top member. Use a square-trimming jig. (See Illus. 7-3.)

4. Cut the rabbets as shown and described in Illus. 7-4 and 7-5.

5. Make the dadoes and grooves. Make the cross-grain dado cuts before cutting the grooves. (See Illus. 7-6.) All of the necessary parts are shown completed in Illus. 7-7. Note that the two sides of the bookcase are not exactly identical to each other.

You can make the grooves for the toe board and the shelf standards in essentially the same way as you make the dadoes. Use an edge guide attached to the router base. (See Illus. 7-8–7-11.)

Complete all the joint cuts—except the back rabbets for the back panel—before assembling the bookcase. You will make the back rabbet cuts after assembling the bookcase.

6. Test the fit of all the parts. Sand all the inside surfaces and assemble the two sides to the top and bottom shelf with six-penny finish nails and glue. Insert the toe board and carefully glue it into its grooves.

7. After all the glue has set, clean up the corner rabbet joints with a flush-trimming bit, as shown in Illus. 7-12.

Illus. 7-3. *First, cut all the boards with a hand or power saw so that they are approximately ⅛ to ¼ inch longer than specified. Then, as shown here, square them to their exact finished lengths. Use a trimming bit that is ball-bearing-guided with a square-trimming jig (described in the previous chapter) to make a perfect end cut.*

Illus. 7-4. *Here, a deep, end-rabbet cut is being made on the top piece of the bookcase. Note that several passes at successively deeper cuts are made to bring the ¾-inch-wide rabbet to its full ½-inch depth. A ¾-inch-diameter, high-speed-steel, straight-cutting bit is being used. The router is guided with an edge guide that is attached to the router base.*

Illus. 7-5. *For the best results, make the rabbet cut about 1/64 inch wider than specified. If you cut the rabbet slightly wider, you can later (after assembling the bookcase) trim or sand the rabbet to make a clean, flush joint. Here the cut is being checked with a scrap that is equal to the thickness of the sides. (See Illus. 7-12 and 7-14.)*

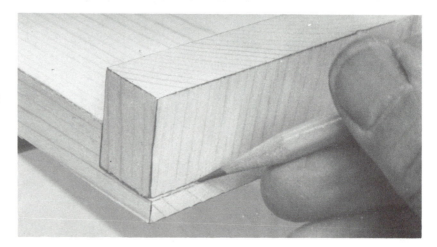

Illus. 7-6. *Making a dado cut on the bottom piece. Here, the edge-guide accessory is being used to make the cut. Note that the edge guide's fence is lengthened by the wood strip attached to it. Depending upon the size of the bit and the router's horsepower, these cuts are made in one or more passes.*

LEFT
SIDE

RIGHT
SIDE

Illus. 7-7 (left). *Next, make the groove cuts for the metal shelf standards and the toeboard. Note that the only difference between the left and right side pieces is in the location of the lower toeboard grooves.*

Illus. 7-8. *Completing the toe-board groove on the right sidepiece. The feed direction is away from the operator.*

Illus. 7-9. *Here is one way to check the depth-of-cut setting when routing the grooves for metal shelf standards. This depth is about ³⁄₁₆ inch. The distance from the bit to the edge-guide fence should be about 1¼ inches.*

Illus. 7-10. *In case you don't have bits with sufficient cutting diameters, make successive passes as required until the correct width is achieved. Always check your adjustments and make a test cut on scrap before making the actual cut.*

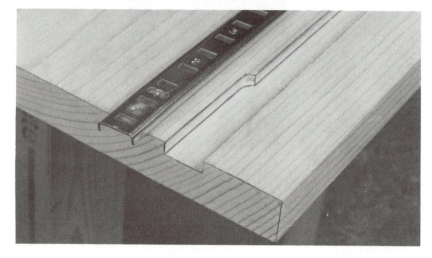

Illus. 7-11. *The grooves for the shelf standards are cut so that when the standards are installed they will be flush to the surface.*

Illus. 7-12. *A trimming bit trims away and smooths any slight overhang on rabbet joints.*

8. Round over all forward edges, preferably with a ball-bearing-guided bit (a one-piece piloted roundover bit will also work). On cuts of this type, where little wood is actually removed, make two or three passes all around at the final bit setting. This will clean up any irregularities that may have been inadvertently missed because the router had been tipped slightly. (See Illus. 7-13–7-15.) Use either a ¼- or ⅜-inch radius roundover bit.

9. Rabbet all around the inside of the rear edges for the back panel. (See Illus. 7-16.) Set the cutting depth of the bit to equal the thickness of the material being used. Remember, *feed the router in a clockwise direction when making these rabbeting cuts.*

10. Once again, sand all over the areas travelled by the pilot. Even though the surface does not show any visible burning or charring, the wood fibres are still somewhat burnished. Telltale lines are likely to show up after these surfaces are stained and finished. This is because these rubbed areas, where the pilot travelled, do not absorb stains and finishes as well as the untouched areas.

11. Stain and finish all the parts of the bookcase.

12. Fit the back panel and secure it with some 1-inch wire nails. (See Illus. 7-17.)

13. Install the metal shelf standards (Illus. 7-18) and adjust the shelf. The bookcase is now complete.

Illus. 7-13. If you round over the inside edges, as shown, the router may tip slightly, one way or the other. This isn't serious. The depth of cut is shallow and is controlled by the pilot and the base. Subsequent sanding will remove minor irregularities.

Illus. 7-14. When you round over the rabbeted end of the top, as shown here, you can eliminate the trimming operation shown in Illus. 7-12 because this bit will simultaneously trim and round over in just the one pass.

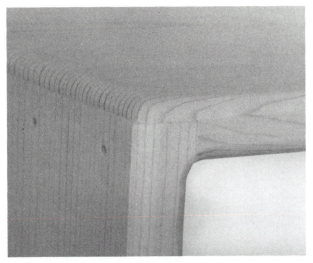

Illus. 7-15. *Here is what the edge-formed corner looks like when a ¼-inch-radius roundover bit is used.*

Illus. 7-16. *Cut the rabbet for the back panel after assembling the pieces. With a little practice, you'll be able to make these cuts safely without tipping the router while making them. The feed should be clockwise, around the inside edges at the back. Do not hesitate or slow down while feeding the router in the inside corner if you are using a one-piece piloted rabbeting bit. If you do, you'll burnish or burn the wood under the pilot.*

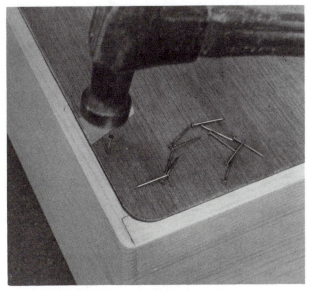

Illus. 7-17. *Either round the corners of the back panel to match the rabbet, as shown, or square-out the corner with a chisel.*

Illus. 7-18. *After you have completed the project, install the shelf hardware.*

Chapter 8

ROUTER TABLES

Router tables have become extremely popular among woodworkers. A router table is simply a router mounted upside down under a flat table surface. When it is being used, the router bit protrudes upwards through an opening in the table.

Various work-feeding guides and accessories can be attached to the table. These guides and accessories can be used individually or in combinations. You can buy commercially produced tables, guides and accessories or make your own. These items include guards, fences, mitre gauges, and vacuum attachments.

You will discover when using a router table that it makes a hand-held router safer and more convenient to use and sometimes improves its performance. Normally, you would move a hand-held router over the stationary workpiece to produce the desired cut. When you use a router table, the router becomes a stationary machine and you can move the workpiece, advancing it properly into the fixed rotating bit to make the desired cut.

Illus. 8-1. *This router table is one of many sold by Sears. It is probably the company's best one. It has a special fence with a work-holding, carriage-feeding system for special operations. It also has guards, a dust-collection hook-up system, a mitre gauge, and a jointer fence.*

Commercially Made Router Tables

Commercially made router tables, like the one shown in Illus. 8-1, are intended primarily for light-duty work. They cost about as much as one of the less expensive routers. Tables like the one shown in Illus. 8-1 are made of stamped sheet metal, aluminum, or plastic ("structural foam"). Some have unique, built-in features that the operator can use to make some unusual cuts that would not be possible with a hand-held router. Remember, these lightweight tables can only be used with light-duty routers. If you eventually decide to use a larger, heavier router, it will not be compatible with your router table. In this case, remember that many mail order companies and tool suppliers offer a variety of heavy-duty router tables that have many accessories and unique features.

Shop-Made Router Tables

Unless you are sure of what size router you will be using and know the exact arrangement of the router table, it is recommended that you build a less expensive one yourself.

Illus. 8-2–8-6 show designs for router tables that you can build yourself. These inexpensive tables can be built very quickly, and will prove to be very functional. The router table shown in Illus. 8-2 and 8-3 should be secured to the edge of your workbench, worktable, or a sawhorse. The router table shown in Illus. 8-5 and 8-6 should be mounted to a wall. It folds out of the way when it is not being used. Both tables have similar constructional features. Illus. 8-4 shows the structural details needed to make these router tables. Note that the table itself is comprised of two layers of wooden sheet material. The top surface is made of ¼-inch-thick tempered hardboard or plywood. A thicker supporting panel (sub-table) is cut out of thick plywood or flake board to surround the router, which drops down through it. This sub-table component is nailed to the one leg of the table shown in Illus. 8-2 and 8-3, or you can screw two hinged legs under the wall-mounted design.

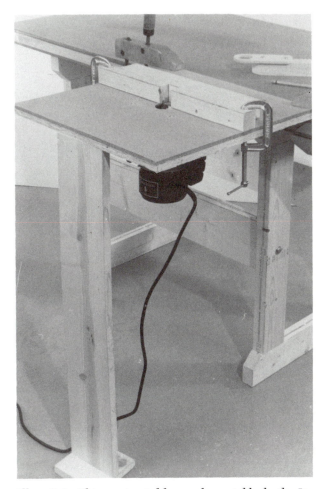

Illus. 8-2. *This router table can be quickly built. It is attached near the edge of a workbench, and is supported by just one table leg.*

Illus. 8-3. *Here's the same router table tacked to a sawhorse. This router table can do the same work many commercially made router tables do. However, when used as shown here, it is set up at an awkward height.*

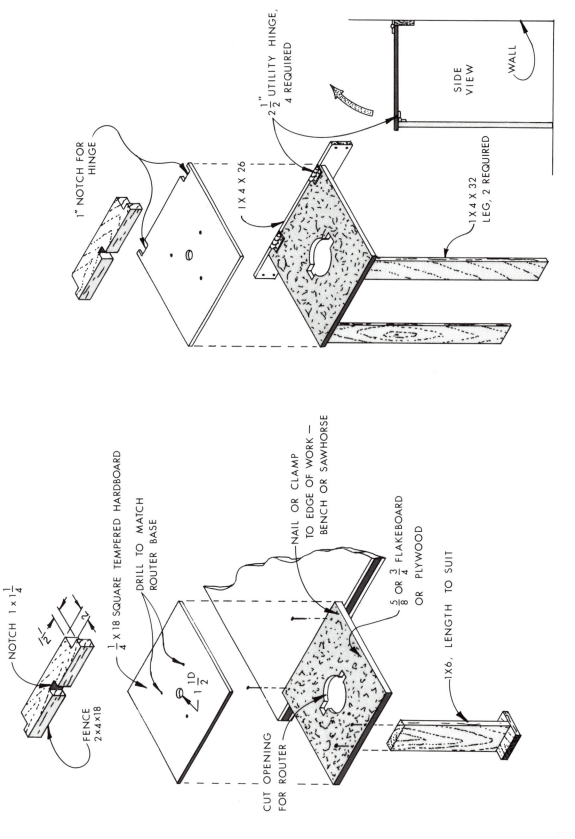

Illus. 8-4. *The construction details for the router tables shown in Illus. 8-2 and 8-3 and 8-5 and 8-6.*

Illus. 8-5. *This wall-mounted router table can be quickly built. This table has two hinged legs, so the entire unit will fold up, out of the way when not in use.*

Illus. 8-6. *Here is the router table in its "up" position, for easy, out-of-the-way storage.*

When you are using the router table, secure the hardboard top surface to the supporting panel under it so that the router doesn't shift around. You can do this in one of two ways. In the first way, you can hold the hardboard top surface and the supporting panel together with clamps when you place them on the edge of your workbench, as shown in Illus. 8-2. Or, if you use the fence (which you will use for most work), you can simultaneously clamp it and the two layers of the table all together, with the clamps normally used to secure it, so that the router is held in a rigid position.

Illus. 8-7–8-18 show and describe every important step involved in constructing the router tables. With a minimum of time and effort and some inexpensive material, you'll find yourself table-routing in less than 30 minutes.

Illus. 8-7. *Step One. Use a piece of plywood or flake board for the sub-table, and a piece of ¼-inch tempered hardboard (or plywood) for the surface. Both should be 18 inches square. Locate the centers of each with diagonals and lay out the sub-base diameter in the center of both pieces.*

Illus. 8-8. *Step Two. Use the sub-base on your router to lay out the screw-mounting holes.*

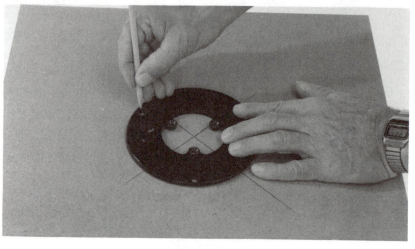

Illus. 8-9. *Step Three. Outline the router base (and other router parts that stick out, such as the handles) on the surface of the plywood or flake-board sub-table, as shown. You can draw the marks with a soft-tipped pen.*

Illus. 8-10. *Step Four. Saw out the outline (top-view profile) of the router.*

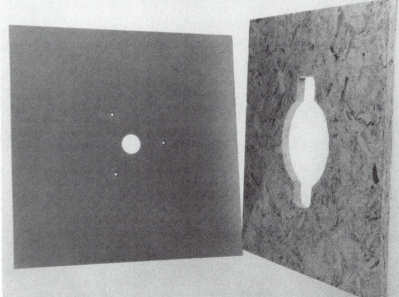

Illus. 8-11. *Step Five. Drill the screw-mounting holes and countersink the screws on the ¼-inch-thick hardboard surface shown on the left. Cut the sub-table piece, shown at the right, to receive any light-duty router.*

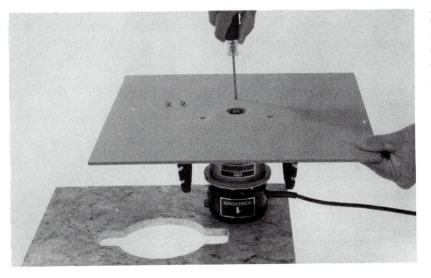

Illus. 8-12. *Step Six. Mount the hardboard to the router as if it is a big, square sub-base. Use the mounting screws from the router's sub-base.*

Illus. 8-13. *Here is another view of the mounted router base. You can mount other brands and styles of routers with removable sub-bases in essentially the same way, if you use the sub-base on those routers as a pattern for the mounting screws.*

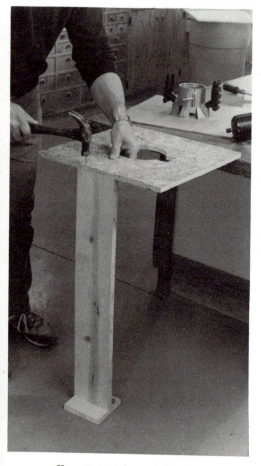

Illus. 8-15. *Step Eight. Slide the router base through the sub-table opening.*

Illus. 8-14 (above left). *Step Seven. Here are the pieces that support the table. In this case, the sub-table has been tacked to the edge of an old workbench and nailed to the leg, which is cut as long as the workbench is high.*

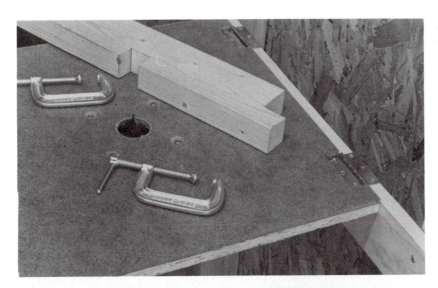

Illus. 8-16. *Step Nine. If you are making the router table that can be folded up, mount it to a solid surface. The router table shown here is mounted to the side of a garage wall. Note the hinges and the matching notches cut into the edge of the hardboard surface piece.*

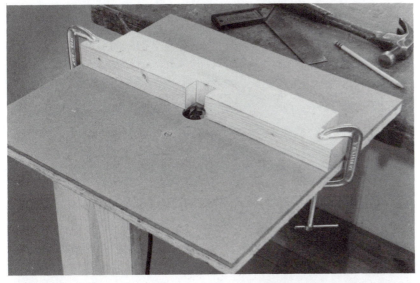

Illus. 8-17. *Step Ten. Cut a straight length of 2 × 4 (a piece of wood 2 inches thick and 4 inches wide) and cut a few notches in it. You now have a good guide fence.*

Illus. 8-18. *The same fence in its optional vertical mode. A fence set up like this gives better support than one resting flat (horizontally) on the table, for feeding workpieces on their vertical edges.*

Routing Techniques

Once you have the router table set up, you will find that you'll be using your router more and more in a table than hand-holding it. Remember, the procedures explored in Chapter 3 still apply here. *It is essential that you always feed the work in a direction that is against the rotation of the bit.* (See Illus. 8-19.) If you find that you have to reach for the switch to turn the router on or off, use an auxiliary foot switch. This permits you to maintain your balance and to keep both hands free for complete control of the workpiece.

Many different edge-forming, decorative, and joint-fitting cuts can be made on the router table. We will take a look at just a few of the more popular and helpful ones.

A fence is used for most straight-line table-routing jobs. (See Illus. 8-19.) Clamp the fence to the table so that its edges are positioned in relation to the *bit* only. It is not at all important how the fence lines up with the edges of the router table; in other words, the fence does not have to be parallel to the edges of the table in order to function properly. (See Illus. 8-20.)

Illus. 8-19. *Shown here is the relationship of feed direction to bit rotation. Also, note that some means must be provided to guide the workpiece. The guide most often used for straight-line work is the fence. Piloted and non-piloted bits can be used with the fence, as shown.*

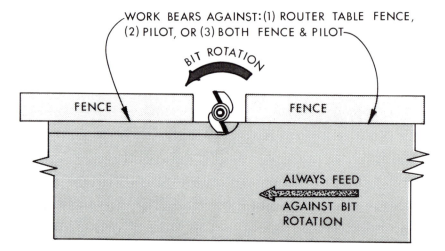

Illus. 8-20. *As shown here, a guide fence does not have to be aligned parallel to the edge of the table. The relationship between the router bit and the fence is the only concern; it is not at all important to have distances A and B equal.*

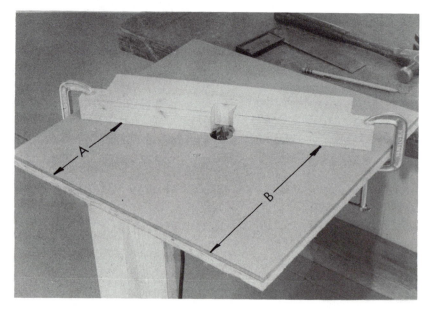

Rabbet Cuts

Rabbet cuts are made the same way as edge-forming and decorative cuts along straight edges. The depth of cut is that distance by which the bit is set to protrude above the table. The horizontal depth of cut depends upon how much of the bit extends beyond the working edges of the fence. As with hand-held work, make as many multiple passes as needed to make bigger, deeper cuts. A small-diameter bit can then be used to produce bigger cuts. (See Illus. 8-21 and 8-22.)

For making a rabbet cut, as with all other types of work, the fence should be adjusted so that it is as close as possible to the bit. The fence can also serve as a guard in many situations.

Illus. 8-23 shows an improper and *dangerous* setup for a rabbet cut. This is the same as feeding with, rather than against, the bit rotation. And, the bit protrudes dangerously alone, well away from the fence.

Illus. 8-23 also shows the rabbet cut with the workpiece being held and fed on its edge. This is also dangerous. A setup that would permit the workpiece to be fed flat on the table (horizontally) is much safer. This is because the workpiece is easier to control; it will not have a tendency to tip when you are feeding.

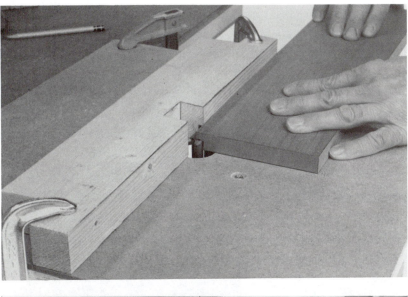

Illus. 8-21. *Basic rabbeting on the router table. (A rabbet is an L-shaped cut made along the edge of the wood.) Note the relationship between the bit and the fence; it controls the horizontal depth of cut.*

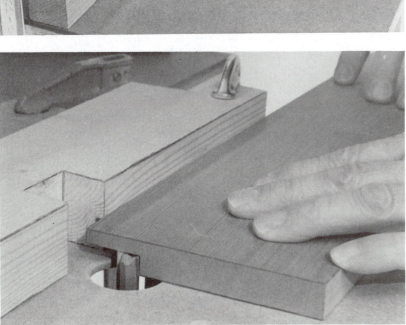

Illus. 8-22. *If you make multiple passes, increasing the distance between the bit and fence each time, you will be able to make wider rabbet cuts.*

Illus. 8-23. *Here's how* not *to set up and cut a rabbet or make other straight-line forming cuts. For obvious safety reasons, you want the bit close to or, when possible, even partially covered by the fence. Never run the workpiece between the fence and the bit.*

Stopped Cuts

Stopped cuts are cuts that do not extend along the full edge of the workpiece. (See Illus. 8-24.) You make a stopped cut without actually seeing the cut being made because it happens on the underside of the workpiece as it is advanced into the router. This is referred to as a "blind cut."

You can predetermine the exact point to stop feeding the workpiece by drawing lines on the fence and on the upper surface of the workpiece. Illus. 8-24–8-28 show and describe how to set up the table, lay out the indicator lines, and make a stopped cut. You can use the same procedures to make stopped edge-forming cuts, stopped dadoes, stopped grooves, and open-end mortises.

Illus. 8-24. *A stopped rabbet cut. Note the layout lines at the end of the rabbet that have been transferred around the edge to the top side of the workpiece.*

Illus. 8-25. *Step One. First, set the depth of cut. Then, set the width of the rabbet cut by adjusting the fence. In this case, a ¾-inch-diameter bit will be set against a straight-board fence to make a rabbet ¾ inch wide.*

Illus. 8-26. *Step Two. Transfer a line from the cutting circle of the bit to the straightedge fence, as shown. This line will be matched up with a line drawn on the top of the workpiece to indicate exactly where the cut is to be stopped. (This is shown in Illus. 8-27.) Since you cannot see the cut being made, you have to depend upon the pre-placed reference lines.*

Illus. 8-27. *Step Three. Start the cut of a stopped rabbet. Note the vertical line marked on the straightedge fence, and the stop-indicator line drawn on top of the workpiece.*

Illus. 8-28. *Step Four. To complete the stopped cut, feed the work forward until both indicator lines meet each other, as shown. Hold the workpiece steady, shut off the power, and wait for the bit to stop rotating before removing the workpiece. The completed cut is shown in Illus. 8-24.*

Tongue-and-Groove Joints

It is not difficult to make the cuts for a tongue-and-groove joint on a router table. Just follow these two steps:

1. Cut the groove component(s) of the joint before making the tongue cuts. Before making the groove cut, set the fence so that the cut will be made as closely as possible down the middle of the workpiece edge. This is because the piece will have to be fed on its edge, as shown in Illus. 8-29. And, to be sure that the grooves are exactly centered, feed the piece twice, once from each end, with each face of the board passing against the fence. This makes both of the cuts the exact-same distance from the bit, and, thus, automatically centers the groove cut.

2. Cut the tongue part of the joint. The tongue can be cut with the workpiece fed vertically (Illus. 8-30) or horizontally, whichever you desire.

Think of the tongue as the result of two rabbets. Plan to cut it slightly shorter than the depth of the groove. This will make the joint fit clean and tight at the surfaces. (See Illus. 8-31.)

Illus. 8-29. *Routing a groove with the workpiece on edge. (A groove is a U-shaped cut. The tongue part of a tongue-and-groove fits into this slot.) To be certain the groove is exactly centered, feed the workpiece over the bit twice, once from each end. This will place each face of the workpiece against the fence, automatically centering the groove.*

Illus. 8-30. *Make the tongue cut in two passes. Lower the bit about 1/64 inch to make the tongue slightly shorter than the matching groove is deep. Check this setup—and any important setup, for that matter—on scrap of suitable size and of equal thickness.*

Illus. 8-31. *A completed tongue-and-groove edge joint. Note that the tongue is slightly shorter than the depth of the groove. This ensures that the joint will be perfectly tight where the tongue and groove meet.*

Jointing

When the edge of a board is jointed, it is made straight, square, and true. You can use a router table to satisfactorily joint a board if you slightly modify the fence and use a straight-cutting router bit. When a router table is set up to joint a board, many woodworkers affectionately refer to it as a "poor man's jointer."

To convert your regular fence to a jointing fence, simply add a piece of thin (¹⁄₁₆-inch-thick) plastic laminate to one half (the out-feed end) of the fence, as shown in Illus. 8-32. The laminate-faced part of the fence is called the "out-feed end"; the other part of the fence is the "in-feed end."

When jointing, make sure that the surface of the laminate-covered end of the fence is exactly in line with and tangent to the cutting circle of the bit. Then clamp the fence exactly at this bit-to-fence location. (See Illus. 8-33.) Bigger diameter bits work best, but jointing will even work with a bit just ¼ inch in diameter. (See Illus. 8-34.)

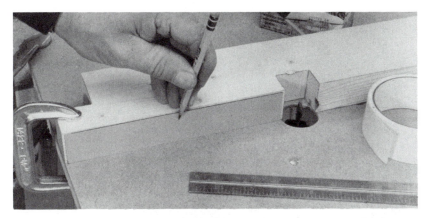

Illus. 8-32. *To make a jointing fence, first bond a piece of ¹⁄₁₆-inch laminate to just one half of the fence, as shown here. Bond the laminate with double-faced tape or contact cement.*

Illus. 8-33. *Next, align the laminate-faced part of the fence to the cutting circle of the bit with a straightedge. The plane (or surface) of this half of the fence should be perfectly tangent to the cutting diameter of the bit. The bigger the diameter of the bit used, the better. Regardless of which size bit is used, the in-feed half of the fence will always be off-set ¹⁄₁₆ inch from the out-feed end of the fence.*

Illus. 8-34. *The jointing operation in progress. Note how the laminate-faced out-feed half of the fence supports the cut edge. Here a ¼-inch spiral bit is being used.*

Alternative Jointing Technique Another way of jointing a board is with a trimming bit (Illus. 8-35) and a straightedge. This technique is similar to template- or pattern-routing, discussed in Chapter 10.

It is easy to joint a board with a trimming bit. Simply attach a straightedge to the workpiece, or attach the workpiece to a straightedge. Place it so that the pilot on the bit will follow the straightedge and cut away whatever material is extending outside the line of cut. If the straightedge is true, the result will be a straight and true jointed edge.

Illus. 8-35 and 8-36 show how to joint a board on a router table with a trimming bit. In this work, the straightedge is mounted directly on top of the workpiece with double-faced tape (tape that sticks on both sides). Leave as little of the workpiece as possible exposed beyond the straightedge to be trimmed away. This is shown in Illus. 8-36. Since the bit has to cut the full thickness of the board, and is so adjusted vertically, the horizontal depth of cut should be minimal, that is, about ⅛ to 3/16 inch per pass.

Illus. 8-35. *This board is being jointed on a router table with a ball-bearing-piloted trimming bit and a straightedge secured on top of the workpiece with nails or double-faced tape. Note the feed direction and the self-made guard.*

Illus. 8-36. *This board, which has a rough-sawn edge, is being jointed with a trimming bit and a straightedge.*

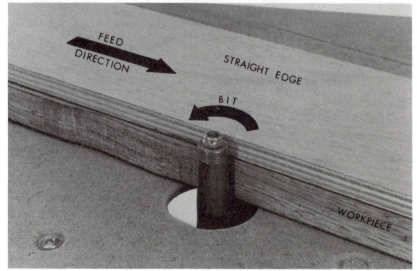

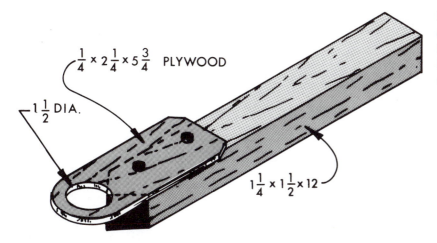

$\frac{1}{4} \times 2\frac{1}{4} \times 5\frac{3}{4}$ PLYWOOD

$1\frac{1}{2}$ DIA.

$\frac{1}{4} \times 1\frac{1}{2} \times 12$

Illus. 8-37. *This homemade guard, also shown in Illus. 8-35, protects the operator when the fence is not being used or when a bit is being used by itself on the table.*

Edge-forming Cuts on the Router Table

You can make edge-forming cuts along and around all straight and curved edges if you use piloted bits. *The key thing to remember is that the workpiece must be fed against the rotation of the bit.* Another factor to consider is that the bit may grab and jerk the workpiece at the start of the cut, unless you are prepared. The bit will grab when it first touches the work, until the cut reaches its full horizontal depth, with the workpiece bearing fully against the pilot of the bit.

To ensure that it is safe to make an edge cut on your router table, clamp a wooden pivot point to the table. This pivot point will be used as a starting block. First, bring the workpiece against the point of the starting block, and then pivot the workpiece towards the rotating bit. (See Illus. 8-38–8-40.) Illus. 8-41–8-43 show how to use and make a push block. A push block is another safety device that should be used in certain edge-forming jobs.

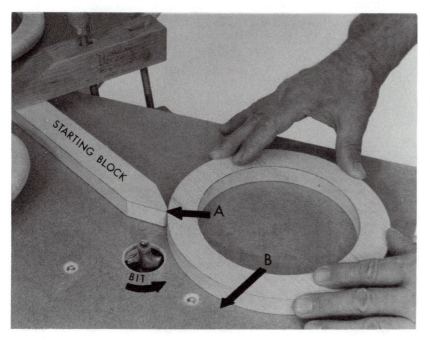

Illus. 8-38. *Rounding over the outside edge of a wooden ring. Begin with the workpiece against the starting block and pivot it carefully into the rotating bit until the workpiece comes to bear against the pilot.*

Illus. 8-39. *Begin feeding the workpiece (in the direction of the arrow) only after you have carefully pivoted it against the pilot of the bit.*

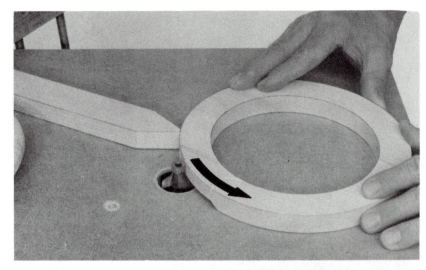

Illus. 8-40. *Here's how the workpiece looks with the guard properly positioned. The workpiece is bearing against both the starting block and the pilot of the bit. Note that the guard circles above the bit, but permits the work to pass under it.*

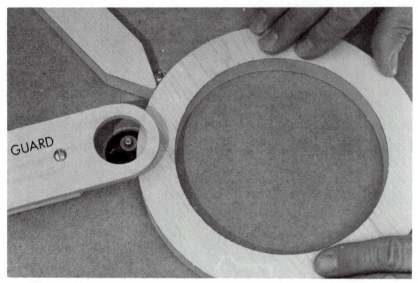

Illus. 8-41. *When you edge-form around the* inside *of a ring, as shown here, you should feed the workpiece in the* opposite *direction from that used when routing around the outside. Note that in this situation, a starting block cannot be used, and the guard will have minimal benefit. Therefore, you should use a special push block, like the one shown here, to safely feed the workpiece.*

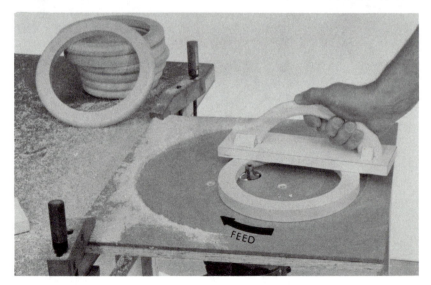

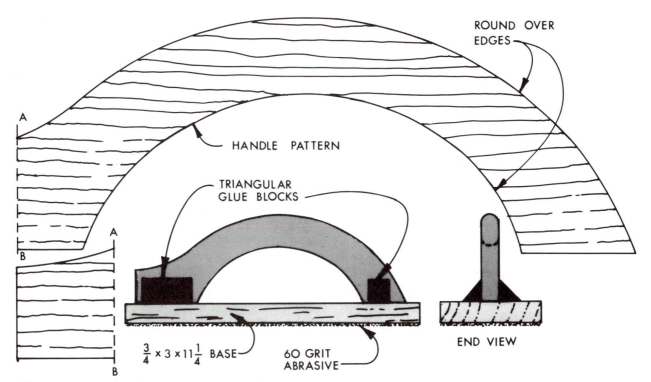

Illus. 8-42. *The details for making a push block for router-table work. This pattern is ¾'s of the actual size of the push block.*

Illus. 8-43. *The push block is best used with two hands, as shown. Apply a downward and circular pressure on it to feed the work into the bit. Withdraw the workpiece from the bit before releasing your pressure on the push block. This way, you can get a new grip on the push block, so that you can feed the uncut edge of the workpiece to the bit. The push block shown here is being used to form an outside edge. It is being used without the aid of a starting block or guard over the bit.*

Squaring and Trimming

You can square and trim a workpiece on a router table if you use an accessory made from just three pieces of wood. This accessory is shown in Illus. 8-44. It functions just like a mitre gauge on some commercially available router tables. Instead of following a groove in the table, this guide has a strip of wood on the bottom that follows along the outside edge of the router table. (See Illus. 8-45–8-47.)

This device was also designed to be adjustable, so it will cut any specific angle if you simply release and reclamp the work support strip using a small C-clamp. Illus. 8-48 shows the router table set up to trim an angle cut.

Illus. 8-44. *The details for making a squaring and end-trimming guide for the router table. This guide is designed to ride against the outside edge of the router table. It functions like the mitre gauge on some commercially manufactured router tables.*

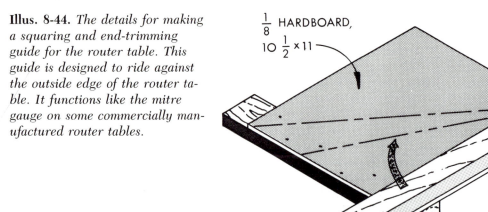

$\frac{1}{8}$ HARDBOARD, 10 $\frac{1}{2}$ × 11

1 × 1 $\frac{1}{4}$ × 14

SINGLE NAIL PIVOT

1 × 2 × 12 $\frac{1}{2}$

Illus. 8-45. *This trimming guide is being used to square the end of a board. The operator is holding the trimming guide against the table edge with his left hand, while simultaneously advancing the workpiece supported on top of the trimming guide.*

Illus. 8-46. *The operator's view of the trimming operation. Note the guard.*

Illus. 8-47. *This closeup look (without the guard) shows a ¼-inch spiral bit removing approximately ¹⁄₁₆ inch of wood while truing and squaring this board end in one pass.*

Illus. 8-48. *Trimming cuts to one edge of the workpiece can be made in various predetermined angles. Here the operator is checking the support strip (stop), adjusted to 60 degrees, by following the edge of the bit with this draftsman's triangle. To adjust the strip, he only has to reposition it and secure the C-clamp to the table edge guide.*

Chapter 9

ROUTING CIRCLES AND ARCS

When you use your router with a commercially available or a home-made circle-cutting jig, it can cut perfect circles. Circular cuts can be used to make wooden wheels, to cut out round holes in projects, and to make round wooden rings, mirrors, or picture frames, to name just a few uses. (See Illus. 9-1–9-3.)

Many different types of jig can be used to cut circles. Here, we will explore three of the sim-plest hand-made jigs that can be used with a plunge router. A plunge router is far easier, more accurate, and generally safer to cut circles with than a fixed-base router. A plunge router is safer because the bit enters the workpiece vertically, with the base set flat on the workpiece. This is just not possible with a fixed-base router. However, experienced router craftsmen regularly make circular cuts with fixed-base routers.

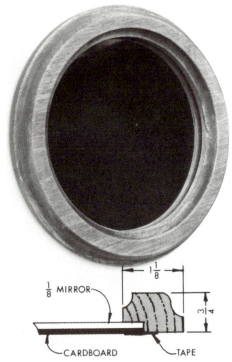

Illus. 9-1. *This wall mirror frame is 9 inches in diameter. You can make one with a diameter of 6 to 11 inches, or even larger, if you desire. Note the typical cross-section details.*

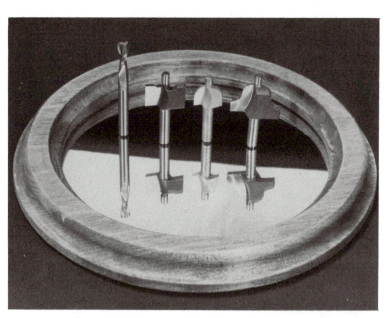

Illus. 9-2. *Here are the bits used to make this wall mirror project. They are, from left to right, a ¼-inch spiral bit, a rabbet bit, a cove bit, and an ogee bit.*

Illus. 9-3. *These rings can be made with any one of a variety of formed edges. They are all rounded over. You can stack and glue them together to make various bowls and vessels, and even use them to make round picture or mirror frames. (See page 104.)*

Trammel Bar

There are many commercially made jigs available. One of the most basic types is sold by Elu. It is called a "trammel bar." (See Illus. 9-4.) You can make a similar type of jig for light-duty work by using a dowel and nail, as shown in Illus. 9-5 and 9-6. You may have to *drill* the nail hole so that you don't split the dowel.

Another, similar jig that can be used to make heavier cuts is shown in Illus. 9-7 and 9-8. However, with this jig, it is not easy to get the nail point located directly over the mark so that it locates the central point of the circle or hole. If you don't want to leave or fill the hole made in the surface by the nail, tape a thin piece of scrap to the surface.

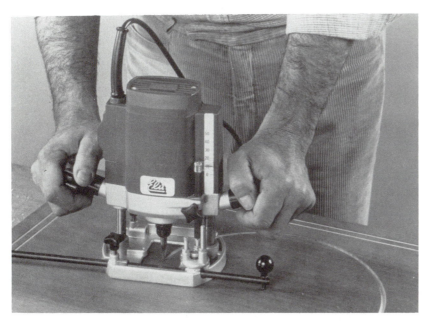

Illus. 9-4. *Elu's trammel bar being used for circle cutting.*

Illus. 9-5. *To make a jig similar to the trammel bar, cut a length of dowel rod and attach it to the router base using the holes normally used for the edge-guide attachment. The radius to be cut is the measurement from the nail to the bit.*

Illus. 9-6. *You can use either a clockwise or counterclockwise feed direction.*

Illus. 9-7. *This jig, designed for somewhat heavier circle-cutting jobs, is also easy to make.*

Illus. 9-8. Circle-cutting jigs such as this one can be made to cut very large circles of any diameter.

Production-Routing Jig

Illus. 9-9–9-12 show a cutting jig designed specifically for production routing of circular discs and rings of various diameters. A small nail for the pivot is driven through the jig at the distance from the bit that equals the radius desired.

This jig, as designed, can be used with a template-guide accessory attached to the router base. The sleeve of the hollow, cylindrical (round) template guide fits perfectly into a hole drilled through a piece of plywood. This is shown in Illus. 9-9.

To make a circular cut, plunge a ¼-inch bit through the template guide and through the plywood jig, as shown in Illus. 9-11 and 9-12. The entire assembly pivots on a nail that acts as a point on this router-powered compass. Also, the router is free to swivel around on top of the plywood jig as the circular motion of the cut progresses. The sleeve of the template guide rotates within its socket-like hole in the plywood jig.

One advantage of this type of circle-cutting jig is that the jig is *not* screwed to the sub-base. You can lift the router off the jig at will, and reposi-

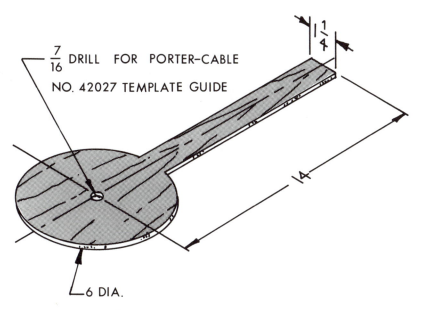

Illus. 9-9. The details for making a circle-cutting jig designed to be used with a template guide mounted in the router base. Note: This type of circle-cutting jig is not intended to be screwed to the base of the router. However, if your router base has no provision for a template guide attachment, then drill holes in the round part and attach the jig directly to it, replacing the sub-base, as shown in Illus. 9-10.

Illus. 9-10. *Attaching the jig directly to the router, replacing the sub-base.*

Illus. 9-11. *This view shows the template guide installed in the base of a plunge router. In use, the barrel or cylindrical sleeve of the template guide fits into a hole of the same outside diameter drilled into the jig. The router pivots around on the sleeve as the entire assembly is rotated in compass-like fashion to make the full circular sweep of the cutting path.*

Illus. 9-12. *Here's a closeup look at the relationship of the plywood jig to the metal template guide sleeve and the protruding bit.*

tion it just as easily by inserting the template guide back into its socket hole.

Illus. 9-13–9-15 show how to set up and use this circle-cutting jig. Illus. 9-16–9-18 show bowls or flower pots that can be made by stacking and gluing the rings that are produced by this type of cut.

It should be pointed out that the details of the jig as specified in Illus. 9-9 can be easily modified to be used without the template guide linked to the socket hole. Simply drill screw-mounting holes to match those locations on your router sub-base. Then screw the circle-cutting jig directly to the base of your router. Depending upon the cutting-diameter size of your bit, you may want to make a bigger hole than specified on the drawing to give more space around the bit.

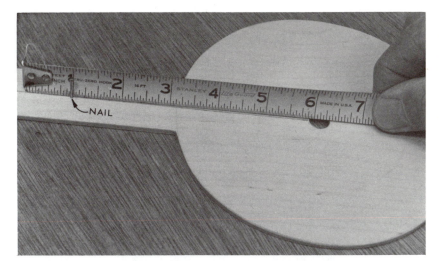

Illus. 9-13. *To make a cut of a specific radius, set the nail pivot point the desired radius from the edge of the jig's hole, plus the offset distance, which is the measurement between the cutting edge of the bit and the outside of the template sleeve, as shown in Illus. 9-12. In this case, that allowance is actually ³⁄₃₂ of an inch.*

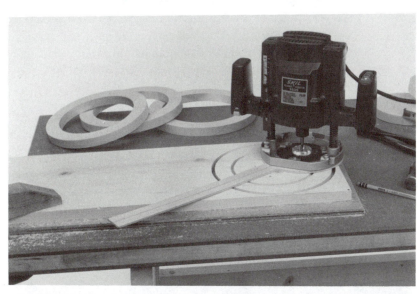

Illus. 9-14. *An overall view showing the setup used to make circular rings. Note the circle-cutting jig and template guide on the plunge router. A ¼-inch spiral bit is being used here. Note that the workpiece is clamped and also nailed to a piece of thin wooden sheet material, supported by a pad of cardboard to protect the surface of the workbench.*

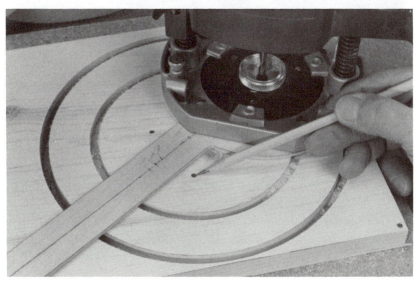

Illus. 9-15. *A closeup look at how the work is nailed and secured so that rings can be cut from ¾-inch-thick pine. Two nails (the pencil is pointing to one of them) secure the central waste piece so that it will not spin when cut free. The board is also nailed on its corners, away from any line of cut, to a pad that, in turn, is clamped to the workbench. This is so that when the bit cuts through the thickness of the wood, freeing the wood pieces, they do not shift and strike the bit. The sawdust in the cut helps to keep the freed ring from shifting.*

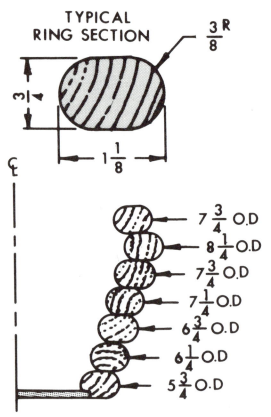

Illus. 9-17 and 9-18 (below). *This bowl-like vessel or flower pot and the ones shown in Illus. 9-18 were made from router-cut rings that were stacked and glued together.*

Illus. 9-16. *Here is a design for one bowl. Given below it are the outside-diameter sizes for various rings.*

Illus. 9-18.

Chapter 10

BASIC TEMPLATE ROUTING

A template is sometimes also referred to as a pattern. Templates and patterns are basically the same. Both are essentially used as a means of guiding the router so that it can cut a particular shape. Patterns and templates are placed onto or under the workpiece, and the router duplicates their contour or profile shapes. For the sake of clarity, the word template will be used throughout this chapter.

When you use a template, you can make contoured cuts that cannot be done with fences and circle-cutting jigs.

Template routing is easy to do. Making the template is usually more involved than actually using it to make the cut(s). (Pages 109–115 explain how to make templates for specific projects.) However, once you try template-routing, you'll quickly realize that this technique can be used to

Illus. 10-1. *The same template was used to make these three different kinds of cut.*

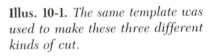

Illus. 10-2. *Some examples of typical templates. These templates were used to make the projects illustrated later in this chapter, and the signboard shown in the next chapter. The heart-and-oval template has two strips attached that center the template over boards cut to a specific width.*

Illus. 10-3. *Template-guided routing to reproduce decorative designs on a door panel.*

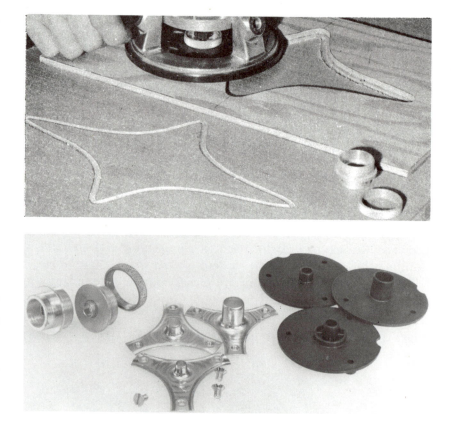

Illus. 10-4. *Three different types of template guides. The guides at left are made by Porter-Cable of machined aluminum. The Sears guides in the middle are made of stamped metal. The guides on the right, manufactured by Skil, are made of plastic. Note the various diameters and lengths of their tubular ends.*

make identical, professional-looking projects over and over in any quantity.

There are commercially made templates available that you can use to make perfect-fitting joints like dovetails or mortise-and-tenon joints, to engrave letters in signs, and other tasks. In this chapter, we will take a look at just a few basic templates that you can make and use yourself.

There are two basic ways of guiding the router along the edge of the template. You can guide the router with a sub-base-mounted "template guide" (Illus. 10-3 and 10-4), or by just using a piloted bit. The most popular piloted bit used is the ball-bearing trimming bit. Each system has certain advantages and disadvantages in different cutting situations and is discussed below.

Template Guides

Template guides are metal or plastic devices that attach to the router sub-base (see Illus. 10-4).

Part of a template guide is tubular, or hollow, in shape. This part extends, or protrudes, through and out from the bottom surface of the sub-base. The bit fits into this tube, and passes through the template guide without touching it.

Of all the brands of commercial template guides available, the most popular are those made by Porter-Cable. They are well made and come in the largest possible selection of sizes. In fact, many router manufacturers have designed or standardized their sub-bases so that Porter-Cable template guides can be fitted to them. (See Illus. 10-5 and 10-6.)

The template-guide system is ideally suited to a variety of surface-cutting jobs, such as those shown in Illus. 10-1 and 10-3. Some jobs, like cutting out a surface recess for a design or making a cut completely through a workpiece to receive an inlay or piercing, are best done with template guides and a plunge router.

It is possible to make these cuts with template guides and fixed-base routers, but it is often very tricky, depending upon the type of cut involved.

When you use a plunge router, you can place the router exactly where you want the bit to first enter the surface. This is often difficult to do with a fixed-base router because you start the cut with the router tilted, and there is an angular bit direction at entry.

Illus. 10-10 shows a typical problem encountered when using a fixed-base router for template-guided routing. Another disadvantage of the template-guide system is that when you are making the template for a project, you have to adjust the size of the pattern. To rout a specific-size profile or design, you must make the profile of the template larger or smaller, to compensate for the distance between the cutting edge of the bit and the bearing surface of the template guide. This is shown in Illus. 10-7–10-9.

Illus. 10-5. This router has a special sub-base insert that is made to carry Porter-Cable's template guides.

Illus. 10-6. The Sears template guide on the left is being mounted on a sub-base. The Porter-Cable guide shown on the right is a two-piece guide that is secured to each side of the sub-base with a knurled, threaded ring.

Illus. 10-7. This Porter-Cable template guide (No. 42027) has a ⁷⁄₁₆-inch outside diameter. When you use it with a ¼-inch-diameter bit, you have to allow for a difference of ³⁄₃₂ inch when designing and making the template pattern.

Illus. 10-8. *This Sears template guide, when it bears against the template, will guide the bit parallel to the edge of the template but at a distance away from it. (See Illus. 10-9.)*

Illus. 10-9. *Here's the resulting recessed heart design that was cut in a pine board with a template guide and a ¼-inch-thick hardboard template. Note that the cut is smaller than the opening of the template.*

Illus. 10-10. *When using a fixed-base router in template-controlled routing, the difficult part is getting the cut started properly. Here the router is tipped on its base and carefully lowered so that the bit will enter as close as possible to the desired location without accidentally cutting into the working edge of the template.*

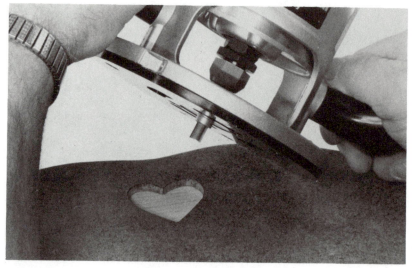

Using Ball-Bearing- or Pilot-Guided Bits

There is an advantage to template-routing with a ball-bearing-guided trimming bit: You can make your template the exact size and shape of the completed part. The disadvantage of this system is that you cannot make vertical plunge cuts. The bit must approach the template and workpiece from a horizontal rather than vertical direction. And, to save time and energy, it's best to first cut the part slightly oversize and just trim the part to its final shape and size with the template and ball-bearing-guided trimming bit. (See Illus. 10-26 on page 116.)

Making Templates

Before you can make a template for the project, determine if you're going to do your routing with a template guide attached to the router base, or just use a flush-trimming bit. If you are going to use a template guide, you have to adjust the size of the template. If you plan to trim a rough-sawn profile using a template and a trimming bit, then cut the template pattern to the actual full size of the completed part or shape.

Templates can be made from a variety of materials. Hardboard ¼ to ⅛ inch thick is perhaps the least expensive, is serviceable and is the easiest material to work. Plywood and plastic are also good choices. The thickness of the material should be compatible with the length of the template guide and/or provide a full ride for the bit's ball bearing or solid pilot. Avoid using soft materials like pine and basswood for templates, especially when using bits with one-piece pilots that require harder materials that resist deforming.

Cut the template out very carefully. Make sure that it has smooth and flowing lines. Trim the straight-line areas with a straightedge and a router. Curves should be cut very carefully and should be free of any dips or irregularities. Every little nick or defect on the template's edge will be reproduced on the workpiece, since the

pilot or template guide faithfully reproduces the guiding edge. (See Illus. 10-10.) Use wood-cutting files or sandpaper backed with a block or dowel to remove any bumps or dips along the working edges of the template.

Once the template has been made, you can reproduce pieces from it in any quantity desired. As discussed before, do not exceed the horsepower, bit sizes, and depth-cutting capabilities of your router. Use the proper safety procedures (Chapter 3) and plan to make successive passes at progressively deeper cuts, as necessary.

Projects

The projects shown in Illus. 10-11 and 10-13 can be made with either a fixed-base or plunge router. These projects are an ideal way for you to gain experience with template-routing. To make the pegboard and sign plaque, cut the profile for the outside shapes with a template pattern and pierce through or just recess the heart designs, as you prefer, with the same template. Read the next chapter for advice on engraving the letters. To make the picture frame projects shown in Illus. 10-13, rout completely through the workpiece to form the inside openings. Illus. 10-17–10-36 show and describe how to make the picture frames, pegboards and signboards.

Illus. 10-11. *This pegboard and sign were template-routed. The outside profile shapes for both projects and the heart design shown in 10-9 were routed with the same template.*

FULL SIZE LETTER PATTERNS

1" GRID SQUARES

FORM EDGES AS DESIRED

PEG LOCATIONS

4 1/4" APART

2"

Illus. 10-12. The plan for the pegboard and signboard, in half scale. ("Half scale" means that what is shown is half the size of the actual projects.) The "welcome" letters are full-size patterns that can be cut out with a scroll saw and applied to the signboard. They can also be engraved into the surface, as shown and discussed in the next chapter.

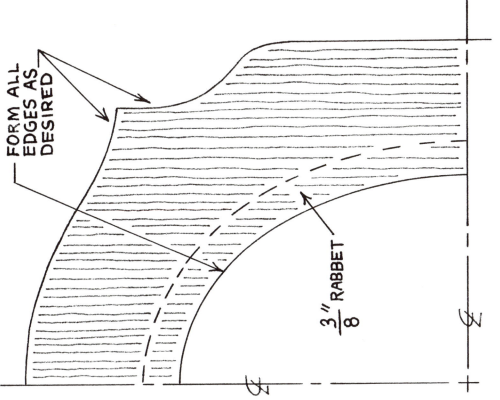

FORM ALL
EDGES AS
DESIRED

$\frac{3}{8}$" RABBET

Illus. 10-14. *A full-size pattern for making 5-inch × 7-inch picture frames. This is a quarter pattern that you must copy and flip on the centerlines to complete the pattern.*

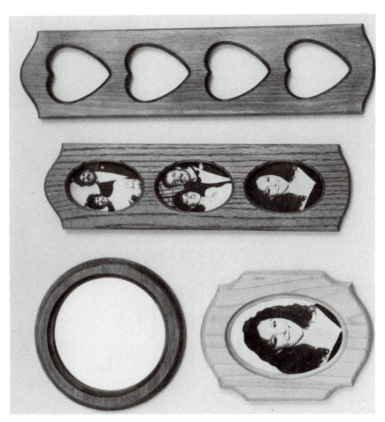

Illus. 10-13. *The perfect circle that makes up the mirror frame on the upper left did not have to be cut with a template guide. These picture frames are best made using templates to produce perfect and identical inside and outside shapes.*

Illus. 10-15 and 10-16 (following page). *Full-size patterns for the snapshot picture frames shown in Illus. 10-13. These patterns are flexible. Make yours with the number of openings that will satisfy your needs. Make the template as shown in Illus. 10-2.*

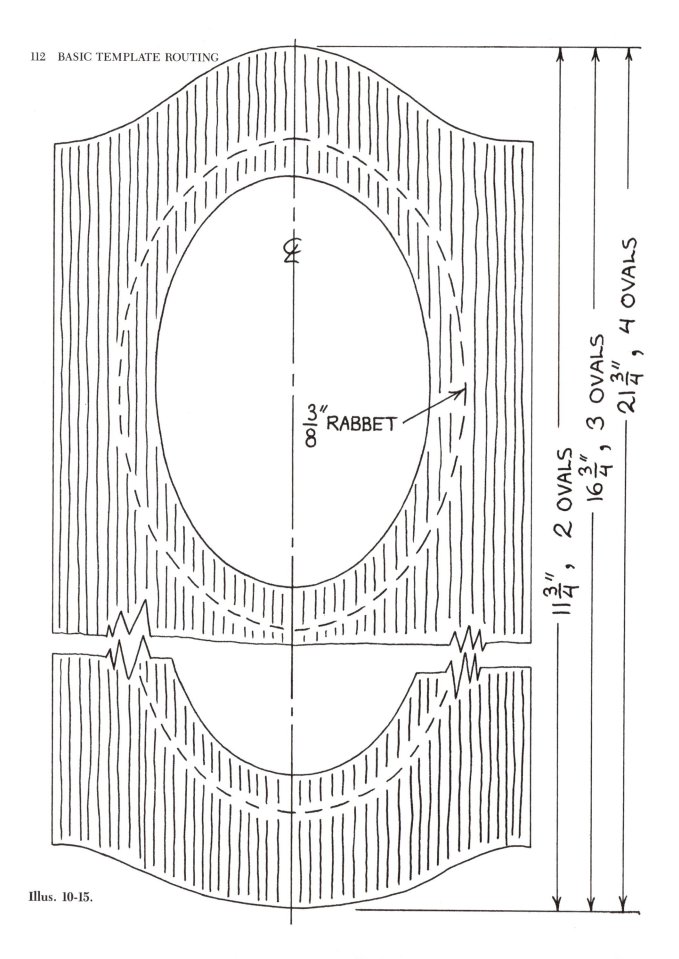

$\frac{3}{8}"$ RABBET

$\mathbb{C}$

$11\frac{3}{4}"$, 2 OVALS

$16\frac{3}{4}"$, 3 OVALS

$21\frac{3}{4}"$, 4 OVALS

Illus. 10-15.

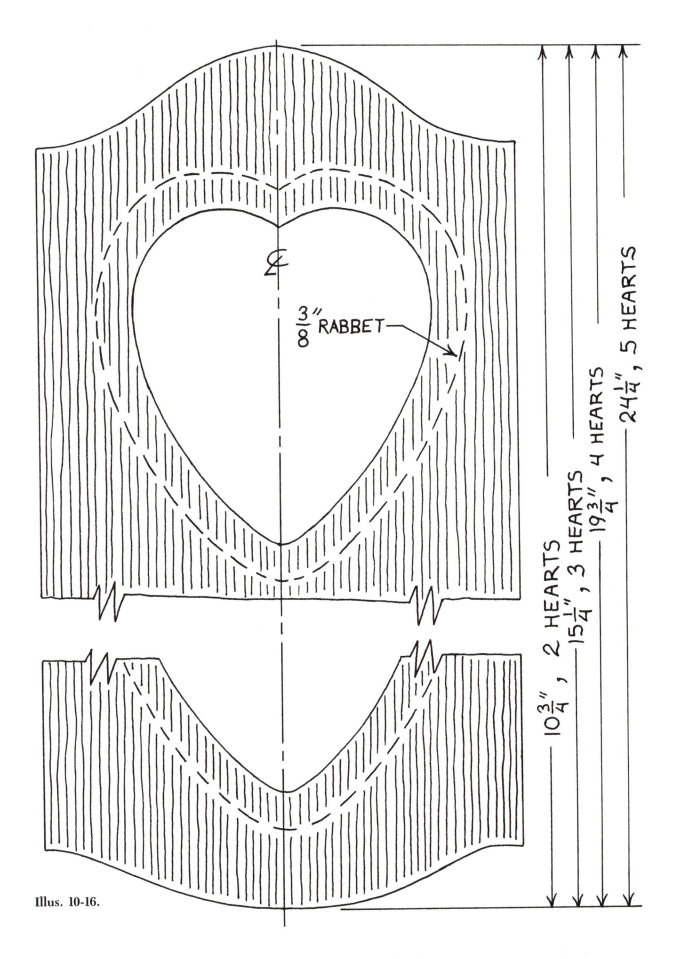

$\frac{3}{8}"$ RABBET

$10\frac{3}{4}"$, 2 HEARTS

$15\frac{1}{4}"$, 3 HEARTS

$19\frac{3}{4}"$, 4 HEARTS

$24\frac{1}{4}"$, 5 HEARTS

Illus. 10-16.

Illus. 10-17. *Step A. Make the template with a scroll saw. Here, ¼-inch-thick tempered hardboard is being cut to make a picture holder template. Note the sharp, accurate layout lines.*

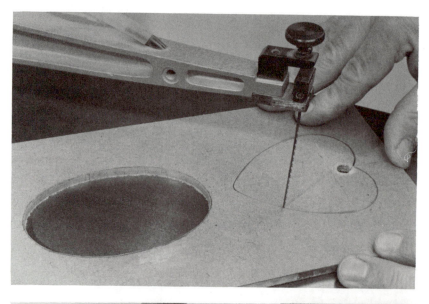

Illus. 10-18. *Step B. Smooth away any dips or irregularities on the contoured edges. This template, used for making the pegboard and signboard, is being touched up with a file.*

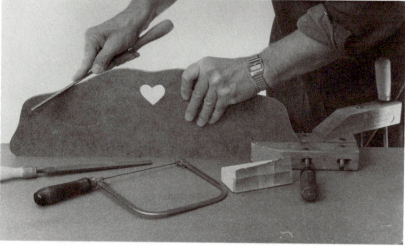

Illus. 10-19. *Step C. Use the template to lay out lines on the wood so that you can saw the piece to its rough size. Later, you will trim it using the same template and a piloted trimming bit.*

Illus. 10-20. *Step D. Saw the project to its rough size, about ⅛ to ³⁄₁₆ inch from the layout lines. Here a hand-held jigsaw is being used to saw the project.*

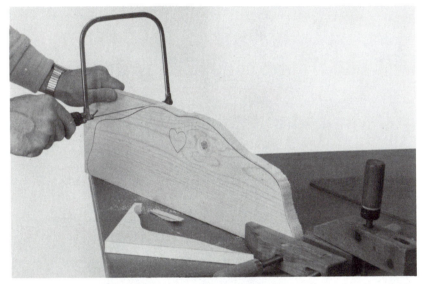

Illus. 10-21. *The very rough cut left by this crude coping saw is of no consequence as long as the project is cut oversize.*

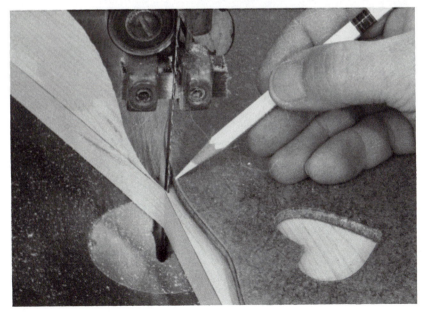

Illus. 10-22. *Some woodworkers like to mount the template directly to the workpiece before sawing the blank attached under it to a rough (larger) size. Here, the blank is being sawed on a band saw. However, if you inadvertently make a mis-cut and saw into the template, you'll not only ruin the workpiece blank, but you'll also have a template that needs repair.*

Illus. 10-23. *A look at the peg/signboard template and the rough-sawn blank.*

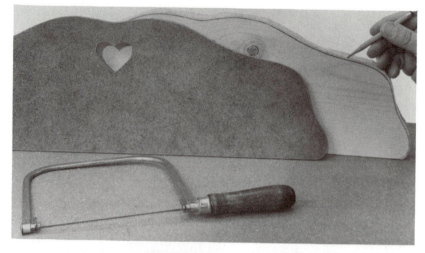

Illus. 10-24. *Step E. Secure the template to the rough-sawn blank with double-sided tape or strategically placed spots of hot melt. Nails can also be used where convenient and where nail holes in the workpiece are not objectionable, as when you are fastening the template to the back, rather than the front exposed side, of the finished project.*

Illus. 10-25. *Step F. Prepare the template and workpiece to be trimmed with a hand-held router. Nails tend to get in the way of the router base, even if they have been driven into the back of the workpiece, so use a couple of pieces of double-faced tape to hold the template against the workpiece for routing.*

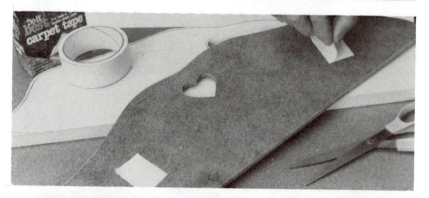

Illus. 10-26. *Step G. Before trimming the template, clamp the work so that the cut is made over the edge of the workbench. Then make the trimming cuts. Note that the template pattern is under the project blank, and that the rough cut is being trimmed down to the template's exact size with a ball-bearing trimming bit.*

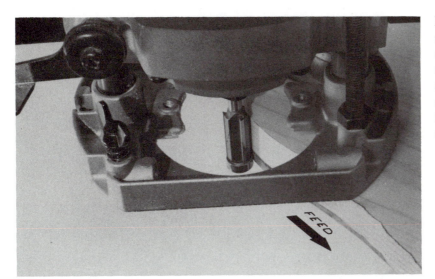

Illus. 10-27. *Step H. Trimming the workpiece. A closeup look at the cutting action. Apply pressure to the workpiece side of the router so that it doesn't tip. A base with a smaller opening would be better. This one does give us an unobstructed view, however.*

Illus. 10-28. *The decorative heart design for the pegboard can be just outlined, recessed, or cut all the way through the workpiece. If using a fixed-base router and a template guide, as shown, make the recess cut to any convenient depth, or pierce through the full thickness of the workpiece.*

Illus. 10-29. *The edges of inside and outside profiles can be easily and smoothly trimmed with a template and a ball-bearing-guided trimming bit.*

Illus. 10-30. *You can add a nice decorative touch to the pegboard if you edge-form around the inside opening of the heart design with a one-piece, high-speed-steel cove bit.*

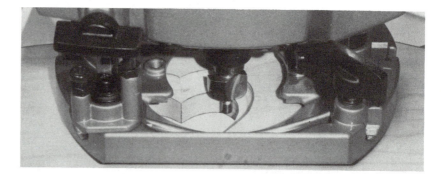

Illus. 10-31. *When template-routing to remove stock to make an opening, set the depth of the bit so that it is just slightly less than what would be needed to cut all the way through. This prevents the freed waste piece from floating loosely against the bit and kicking back with force. To remove the waste piece, cut it free with a sharp knife, as shown.*

Illus. 10-32. *Rabbeting the backs of the picture frames. Note the clamp holding the work to the workbench.*

Illus. 10-33. *This picture frame project is an ideal one on which to practise template routing on a router table. First, saw out the blank so that it is about ⅛ to 3/16 inch larger than the project. Next, nail the template to the back surface. The two nail holes in the back will not be visible on the finished project.*

Illus. 10-34. *Trimming the inside oval of the picture frame to its exact size on the router table. Feed the piece clockwise for the inside work, as shown, and clockwise when trimming the outside profile. When making inside cuts, as shown here, never place your hands inside the piece, regardless of how much space you might have. To minimize the tendency of the bit to grab at the start of the cut, begin the cut by approaching the side-grain area, rather than starting in an end-grain area at the top and bottom of the oval.*

Illus. 10-35. *A closer look at the bit's cutting action and its relationship to the workpiece feed.*

Illus. 10-36. *Each template-produced picture-frame blank is an exact copy in size and shape of the previous one.*

Illus. 10-37. *The project and the bits used. All edge-forming jobs can also be performed on the router table. This frame has a cove formed around the inside of the oval, a rabbet around the back, and a round-over around the outside face profile edges. Note the metal hanger and the two nail holes in the back resulting from attaching the template to the workpiece.*

Chapter 11

FREEHAND ROUTING

Freehand routing is any cut made without the guidance of a device or some mechanical means to control the direction of the router. Accessories such as edge guides, straightedges, fences, templates or template guides, or special jigs and piloted bits *are not used* in freehand routing. It's just you and the router!

On some jobs it is impractical to use jigs. These jobs can only be accomplished freehand. The job shown in Illus. 11-1 is a typical example. It would be impossible to efficiently design and cut the templates necessary to make all of the different kinds of cut required.

Some types of freehand work are easier to do than other types. For example, it is difficult to completely cut a line that's part of a design in just one single pass of the router. (See Illus. 11-2.) It is not so difficult to engrave the letters in a signboard project. (See Illus. 11-3.)

There are many factors involved in successfully freehand-routing work. They include the following: 1, the size, style, and sharpness of the bit; 2, the type of router and its horsepower; 3, the characteristics of the wood itself; 4, the

Illus. 11-2. *Each line on this piece was made with just one pass of the router. When freehand-routing lines in one stroke, be very careful: Any misguided cut will destroy the character and features of the design.*

Illus. 11-1. *Some freehand work on a large sign by Bob Spielman.*

Illus. 11-3. *These engraved letters were routed in multiple passes. The design of the letters made the job easy. The lines of the letters did not have to be perfectly straight, uniform in width, nor exactly identical to each other, yet the overall appearance and effect of the sign is good. (Refer to page 126 for the letter patterns necessary to make this project.)*

depth of cut; 5, the simplicity or complexity of the design; 6, the visibility of the bit; and 7, the physical strength of the operator.

Freehand routing can be fun if you approach it realizing that it takes some practice to gain the necessary skills. Expect to make some misdirected cuts.

Generally, you'll have more freehand-routing control if you use small-diameter bits with a heavy router that has more horsepower. Use carbide-tipped or solid carbide bits, especially when you have to feed the router slowly. In fact, sometimes it's almost easier to control slow, deep cuts than fast, shallow ones. If you feed slowly, as all beginners need to do, you'll overheat high-speed-steel bits and dull them quickly—much more so than carbide bits. Experienced freehand router craftsmen, however, will use high-speed-steel bits because they are very sharp. Experi-

enced craftsmen also feed the router very quickly into the workpiece, and prefer to work with materials such as redwood, which machines easily.

Most router sub-bases are not ideally suited for freehand work. Use a sub-base with a large central hole so that you can see what is going on all around the bit. You may elect to remove the factory sub-base and replace it with a self-made version that provides maximum visibility. This is a situation in which it is nice to have a transparent plastic base.

Make some practice cuts in scrap before undertaking an important project. It's important that you know how the router feels and moves when it starts up, and when the bit passes through the wood in different directions to the grain.

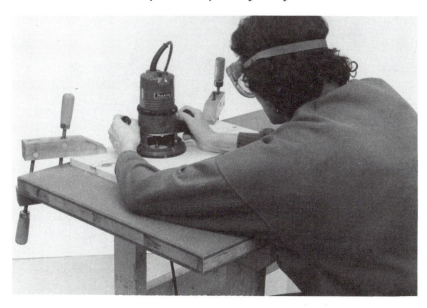

Illus. 11-4. *Here is the proper way to freehand-rout. The workpiece is securely clamped and well back on the workbench, so that the operator's arms rest on the bench and are fairly outstretched. The operator is seated so that he has a good view of the cutting bit. Note the goggles. Always use goggles for any job.*

Make sure you are set up comfortably. (See Illus. 4.) Generally, it's best to be sitting, but this actually depends upon the size of the job and the height at which you must work the wood. Illus. 11-4 shows how and where to clamp the workpiece on the workbench so that it is in the best location for routing.

Make practice cuts on the face of a piece of inexpensive softwood, such as pine. (See Illus. 11-5.) These cuts should run in different directions. You will quickly learn, as mentioned, that there are many factors that influence how successfully you make the cut. Two of these factors—the speed and rotation direction of the router bit—remain constant. Factors that constantly change, however, are the feed speed, the direction the router is moved, and the way the bit cuts in relation to the grain direction.

By looking at Illus. 11-5, you'll note that the router will stray away from its intended course and go in another direction when fed in different angles to the grain of the wood. Study this illus-

tration so that you can anticipate what the router will do when you freehand-rout.

It's usually best to move the router in a direction that will tend to pull the router away from rather than towards or into a straight line. (See Illus. 11-6.) Also, try to make cuts from a top-to-bottom feed direction; that is, make a cut across a board by starting at the farthest point and pulling the router towards you. This is called a "downstroke."

It is easier to control a router by making a downstroke than trying to make the same cut by pushing the router away from yourself—called an "upstroke." You'll find that it is easiest to feed the router on a downstroke at approximately a 45 degree slant to the right. The router almost follows a straight line by itself in this direction. The most difficult feed is directly the opposite—an upstroke, 45 degrees to the left. Try to avoid this stroke whenever possible.

Although it's more time-consuming and slows the job, you can make better cuts by unclamping

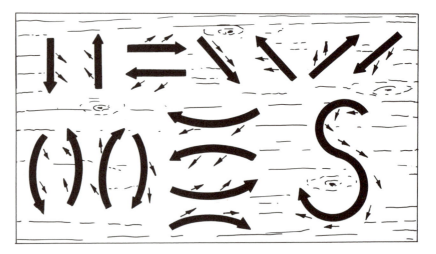

Illus. 11-5. *Shown here are strokes you should practise, and the wandering tendencies of the router when it is fed in various directions in wood with horizontal grain. The large arrows are the intended feed directions. The small arrows indicate the direction the router tends to go if it is not physically restrained.*

Illus. 11-6. *This workpiece is ready for freehand routing. It is laid out with sharp, but dark, pencil lines and clamped tightly to the workbench. The factory sub-base is not being used. Instead, a special self-made sub-base designed to give maximum visibility around the bit, has been substituted.*

the board and reorientating it on the bench so that you can make most of the cuts with a pulling downstroke, rather than with a pushing up-stroke.

Illus. 11-7–11-18 show and describe a technique for routing a typical sign with engraved-style letters. Essentially, the process involves making an initial narrow pass through the middle of the letter and then widening it with successive passes until you have routed to the layout line(s). The same process can be applied to rout out various other designs, such as hearts, animal profiles, etc. In all cases, first rough out the central area and then gradually increase the cuts, cutting little by little outward towards the layout line.

You may need to make several slow final passes, all from the same direction, until all the waste is cut away.

You'll no doubt find occasion to repair a mis-cut, as shown in Illus. 11-14. You can often correct such mis-cuts simply by "fairing out" the line, that is, reworking and smoothing out the cut line so that it flows gradually back into the course of the original. (See Illus. 11-14–11-16.)

As you gain experience, you'll begin to move the router faster, with more confidence and skill. At this time, try some single-stroke work, such as outlining various designs in one continuous pass with the router, or routing letters in a single stroke.

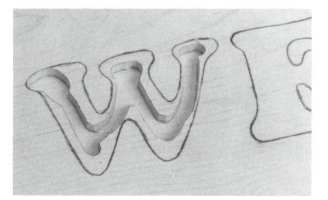

Illus. 11-7. Routing a sign with engraved letters. Set a ¼-inch straight-cutting bit at a cutting depth of ³⁄₁₆ inch. Make one pass down the approximate middle of the letter. Try not to touch the layout line.

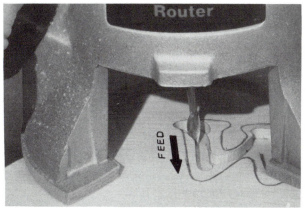

Illus. 11-8. Slowly widen the cut by working on the left side of the previous pass with a downstroke (that is, pulling the router towards you).

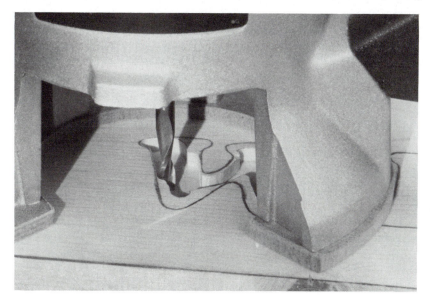

Illus. 11-9. Remember the following rule until you develop a "feel" for the cut: The maximum width of each successive stroke (pass) should not be greater than half the diameter of the bit.

Illus. 11-10. *To widen the cut, use as many strokes or passes as necessary until you meet the layout line.*

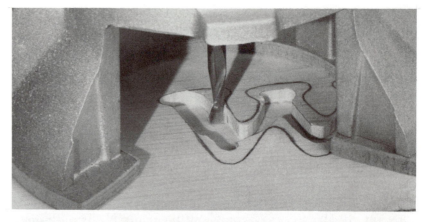

Illus. 11-11. *Making a horizontal cut with the grain, on the bottom of the letter E. It's best to reposition the workpiece under the clamp so that you can use a pull stroke. Again, work on the left side of the previous cut, progressively working towards the left until you meet the line.*

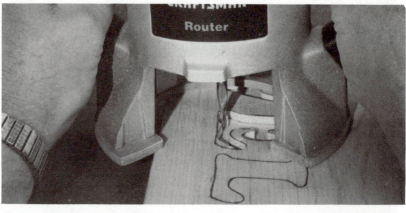

Illus. 11-12. *Reclamp the workpiece or position yourself so that you can make horizontal cuts with a pull stroke, such as on the top of the letter E, as shown here.*

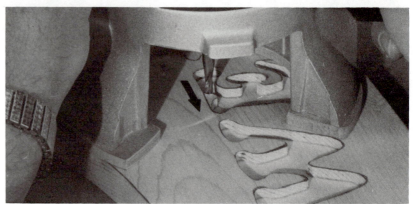

Illus. 11-13. *Look at your work. If the cut is not widened all the way to the line but the overall shape of the letter looks good, then leave it as it is. Removing this slight uncut amount isn't worth the risk of cutting away more than intended.*

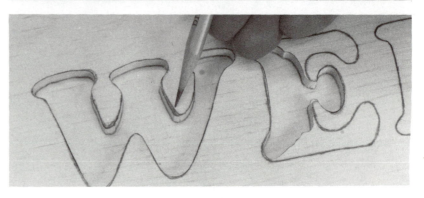

Illus. 11-14. If you accidentally cut beyond the line, as shown here, you can rework the shape of the letter by "fairing it out." (See Illus. 11-15.)

Illus. 11-15. If you fair out the line with a new trimming cut, as indicated by the arrow, the outline of the letter will appear smooth and flowing again.

Illus. 11-16. The touched-up letter may not be perfect, but it is definitely improved and will not stand out. You can fair out almost all lines, whether they are curved or straight.

Illus. 11-17. Complete the sign routing by forming a decorative edge all around the outside with a piloted bit. This class of routing is far more foolproof than freehand work.

Illus. 11-18. *You can enlarge these letters and numbers on a copy machine to make any size sign desired.*

Index

A
Arcs, routing techniques for, 98–104
Auxiliary sub-bases, 52–53

B
Ball-bearing-guided bits, 108
Bases, 7, 19–21
Bead, 24
Bevel, 24
Bits
  care and maintenance of, 31–33
  changing, 22
  definition of, 6, 7
  installation of, 43–45
  materials for, 23
  selection of, 34
  sharpening, 33
  types of, 23–31
  when edge-forming, 51
Bookcase, making, 70–77
Brazing, 24

C
Carbide, 24
Chamfer, 24
Circles, routing techniques for,
  98–104
Clamping and locking mechanisms,
  14, 16–18
Collet, 7, 14, 15
Collet wrenches, 22
Concentric, 7
Cord, router, 22
Core box bit, 24
Cutters. *See* Bits
Cutting diameter, 24
Cutting edge length, 24
Cutting guidelines, basic
  practice cuts, 48
  setting depth of cut, 45–48
  for straight-line surface routing,
    51–52

D
Dado, 24, 25
Depth of cut
  definition of, 7, 41
  setting, 45–48
Dust collection piece, 39
Dust mask, 35

E
Ear plugs, 35
Edge-forming
  bits for, 51
  definition of, 10
  on router table, 93–95
Eye protection, 35

F
Feed direction, 41, 48–51
Feed rate, 24, 41, 48–51
Fences, 86
Fixed-base router, 7–12, 16–17

Flute, 24
Foot switch, 36
Freehand routing, 120–126

G
Grooves, 24

H
Handles, 18–19
Hardwood, 24
High-speed steel, 24
Horsepower, 22

J
Jigs
  production-routing, 100–104
  for straight and square cuts, 64–65
Jointing, 91–92

K
Keyhole bit, 24

L
Laminate trim bit, 24
Letters, engraved-style, 122–126

M
Mortises, 24
Moulding, 41

P
Pegboards, making, 109–119
Picture frames, making, 109–119
Pitch, 24, 32
Plunge routers
  clamping and locking mechanisms
    of, 17–18
  description of, 7, 9, 13–14
Plywood, 24, 41
Practice cuts, 48
Production-routing jig, 100–104
Push block, 93, 95

R
Rabbet bit, 24
Rabbet cuts, 87–88
Resin, 24, 32
Revolutions per minute (RPM), 7
Roundover bit, 24
Routers. *See also specific types of
    router*
  buying, 22
  knowing how it works, 40–43
  parts and features of, 14–21
  type of, 6, 7–14
Router tables
  commercially made, 78
  definition of, 7
  edge-forming cuts on, 93–95
  shop-made, 79–85
Routing techniques
  for circles and arcs, 98–104
  for edge-forming cuts, 93–95
  fences and, 86
  for jointing, 91–92

for rabbet cuts, 87–88
squaring, 95–96
for stopped cuts, 88–89
for tongue-and-groove joints, 90
trimming, 95–97
RPM (revolutions per minute), 7

S
Safety techniques, 35–39
Self-guiding bit, 24
Shank, 7
Sheet plastic, 41
Signboards, making, 109–119
Slots, 24
Softwood, 24
Specialty bits, 31
Spindle lock, 7
Spiral bits, 24
Square base, auxiliary, 64–65
Square cuts, making, 64–69
Square-trimming guide
  making, 64
  using, 66–69
Squaring, 95–96
Stopped cuts, 88–89
Straight cuts, making, 64–69
Straightedge, 41
Straightedge guide, 7
Straight-line surface routing, 51–52
Sub-bases
  auxiliary, 52–53
  description of, 7, 19–21
  freehand routing and, 121
Surface-cutting bits, 23, 25
Switches, 18–19

T
Tempered hardboard, 41
Template-routing
  ball-bearing-guided bits for, 108
  basic, 105–119
  making templates, 109
  projects for, 109–119
  template guides for, 106–108
Templates
  definition of, 105
  making, 109
Tongue-and-groove joints, 24, 90
Trammel bar, 99
Trimming, 95–97
Try square, 7
T-square guide
  making, 64
  using, 65–66

V
Vibration, 22

W
Workbench
  description of, 40
  making, 54–63

Z
Zeroing out, 41

Other Books by Patrick Spielman

Alphabets and Designs for Wood Signs

Carving Large Birds

Carving Wild Animals: Life-Size Wood Figures

Gluing and Clamping

Making Country-Rustic Wood Projects

Making Wood Decoys

Making Wood Signs

Realistic Decoys

Router Handbook

Router Jigs & Techniques

Scroll Saw Country Patterns

Scroll Saw Handbook

Scroll Saw Fretwork Patterns

Scroll Saw Fretwork Techniques and Projects

Scroll Saw Pattern Book

Scroll Saw Puzzle Patterns

Spielman's Original Scroll Saw Patterns

Victorian Scroll Saw Patterns

Working Green Wood with PEG